Broken, but not Beyond Repair

An Exploration to Find Inner Joy and Peace

By Karen Holder

First Printed in United Kingdom 2018

Published by Conscious Dreams Publishing

www.consciousdreamspublishing.com

ISBN: 978-1- 912551-27- 9

Dedication

This book is dedicated to my amazing Auntie Delilah Yvonne Toppin, who lost her battle with cancer on 29th October 2017.

She was an amazing God-fearing woman and was faithful to God until the end. Even though she was taken from us too soon, her memory and legacy shall live on. I know that you are at the right hand of your Father and now resting peacefully in his arms. I love you so much and I will never forget all of the fun times and laughter we shared together.

I would also like to dedicate the book to my mother who has been a pillar of strength to me throughout my life. I am so blessed to have you as my mother and I hope that I have made you proud. I thank you for all that you have done in my life and continue to do for me as well as believing in me and supporting me on my journey. I can never repay you.

Acknowledgements

There are too many people to acknowledge, but firstly, I would like to thank God as He deserves all of the glory. Without knowing God and having a relationship with Him this book would not have been possible. He has shown me the light and allowed me to grow into the person that I am today. You are great and worthy to be praised.

To my daughter, Cadene, I am truly blessed to have you in my life and grateful that God allowed me to be your mother. You have taught me a great deal over the years, in particular the art of patience, but I also appreciate the support and encouragement you have given me on my journey in writing this book. You are an amazing young lady. Love you to infinity and beyond.

I have a great network of friends and family that have supported me and been consistent in my life. I would like to thank them for believing in me and encouraging me to pursue my dream of becoming an author. I am also very thankful that God created the path to connect me with the right people to enable this to happen.

Throughout my journey there are many people that witnessed me going through difficult situations. These people not only prayed for me but walked alongside me even when I wasn't a pleasure to be around. I have not called you out individually as this would be far too great a list but you know who you are and I would like to thank you for not giving up on me and helping me to become the woman I am today. I pray that God will continue to watch over you and strengthen you throughout your own journeys.

Thank you to all those at Conscious Dreams publishing that helped my dream become a reality and believing in my story.

What People Are Saying About
Broken, Not Beyond Repair

"It is an honest account of your life, your relationship with God, and because of this it drew me into reading further to find out how you conquered your demons. I liked the first paragraph of your conclusion, the fact that you were broken, continuing to repair and will come across obstacles. Another honest point is that although you have God in your life, not everything is perfect, but a work in progress. I am really proud of you and look forward to purchasing this and many other books to follow."

– Anthea Hawley

"I like the analogy of the umbilical cord and being connected to God and the use of Scripture within the chapters."

– Serena Holder

"It was very engaging and an interesting read."

– Barbara Asiedu

"I found the chapters relatable and liked the examples that were used. You are amazing."

– Paula Perry, Cycle-Breaking Coach and Author

Contents

Contents

Introduction

"The life in front of you is far more than the life behind you. Every morning has a new beginning. A new hope. It's a perfect day, because it's God's gift." – Joel Osteen, Pastor (Lakewood Church)

We have all been there, felt broken emotionally, physically, mentally and spiritually.

This book may help you overcome those feelings of brokenness and let you know that you are not alone and can be repaired. You may ask what makes me so special and gives me knowledge or authority to talk on this subject. I am not special at all, but my journey has taught me how to cope and to develop into a better person, the person God created me to be. However, I am still a work in progress. Although not complete I am being repaired along the way.

Throughout my journey, I have learnt to lean on God who has given me the strength, courage, peace and tenacity to continue. I have made considerable progress and my friends and family can actually vouch for that, as they know how far I have come. God has reshaped me, repairing the broken pieces, and shown me that although I may be broken, I am not beyond repair. Don't get me wrong, I am not totally repaired or perfect. Who is for that matter? But I am being restored and renewed daily. The same, I believe, applies to all of us and hopefully some of you may be able to relate to my journey and apply God's principles in your life to help you to heal. This book may not even be for you but may benefit someone you know who is struggling with depression, low self-esteem or anxiety and can see no future ahead. I just hope it reaches you at the right time. Although I am revealing some of my life to you and being vulnerable to complete strangers, I believe this is something that God has ordered me to do. Therefore, I cannot be disobedient to

Him. As well as sharing some of the situations that occurred in my life, the book provides chapters that I believe will challenge you. This is an aid to help you overcome your difficulties and handle your emotions better. There are exercises you can carry out, looking deeper into yourself even if it may be hard. I believe that they will help you gain a better understanding of yourself. Releasing you from captivity and breaking chains allowing you to step into a better future. This book is about me and some of the things I have experienced on my journey, but is also a support for you to use in the hope that it will encourage you to become the person you are truly meant to be.

I know of many people that have gone through more traumatic experiences than myself. I have developed a deep admiration for them as I have watched them overcome these adversities. In fact, my story is probably just a drop in the ocean compared to theirs. However, it is still my story, my journey and I have been taught not to discount it as it is still important and I believe could make a difference in someone's life. Therefore, you should not discount yours either and I hope that one day you will find the courage to share it to help others that have been through or are going through a similar journey to you.

I pray that *Broken, Not Beyond Repair* will give you new hope and inspire you to make the necessary changes to create a better and new you!

Where it all began

I remember standing in the school playground between the age of eight or nine with a bible in my hand. It was a small red bible with a soft leather cover that I had taken from home, and whilst others were playing I was busy reading about Adam and Eve. A couple of children came over to me and I was trying to share with them all that I was learning. They, however, seemed to be more interested in running around, playing kiss chase and hopscotch rather than listening to what

I had to say. I suppose that was my first ever attempt of evangelising and I wanted my peers to get excited in the same way that I was, but that failed miserably.

As a child, I had felt a little bit ostracised and never felt that I actually fitted in anywhere. Although I had siblings, I always felt a little different. Being the youngest of three, I was always viewed as my brother and sister's younger sibling and felt that I was accepted just because of that. Sometimes I did silly things to be noticed, but then I suppose most children do and I probably wasn't alone. We also moved home when I was seven. We had been living in temporary housing for some time and were eventually re-housed in a three bedroomed home in Fulham. I then had to make new friends at my new school. I found this pretty difficult, especially when children had already formed bonds with one another before I had arrived. I was also very shy so this didn't help very much either. I was the child that was left to hold the hand of the awkward person that nobody else liked during school outings. I was that child that had no true friends, the hanger on, the one who often got bullied and was taken for granted. The child that would do things to please others, compromising who I was just to be accepted, even if it left me hurting on the inside.

I was a very shy child and if someone spoke to me too sternly I would run off in a flood of tears. To enable myself to look stronger I felt the need to build up a façade to protect myself and pretend that I was ok. After a while of being bullied, it's sad to say that at some point during secondary school I became a bit of a bully. This made me feel strong and also prevented people from picking on me. School life wasn't particularly great for me but I had nowhere to turn and no one that I could truly confide in with my fears and concerns. So, I suppose for that brief period of time in primary school I looked to the Bible to seek my comfort. Maybe that was the first time I was truly reaching out for God to help me.

That is why I am inspired to write this book, I am not claiming to know the answers to everything, but I have managed to make it into my forties with these issues looming over me. I have been able to find a way to cope and make it through even when I felt the odds were against me. I only hope that the words I am writing can help others overcome situations and hurdles that they are faced with through life.

I want to share with you some of my story and the things that my walk with God has inspired me to write, as well as the Scriptures that I have picked up along my journey. Sometimes I wondered why He would wake me up in the dead of the night to write songs and questioned what the purpose was. I would often ask Him, "Why would You make me write songs if I am not given an opportunity to sing them?" I have had a few occasions at my local church where I have been able to speak and also share some of these songs. I was then told by some of the members how my words or songs had inspired them and helped them with their struggles. At one point, a member of the congregation spoke to me and said I should write a book. Maybe she planted the seed without me knowing or was actually prophesying over my life. God had answered me by letting me know that my words and songs had impacted these people, even if this was only a handful. But I also believe that He wants me to reach out further to people and impact them in the same way through writing this book.

I am certain that a lot of people have experienced difficulties in their lives and I am not claiming that my issues are any different from yours. The Bible says that the Lord will only give you as much as you can bear. I constantly question this scripture and I'm sure you would agree with me when I say I would prefer not to bear anything at all, thank you very much! Life isn't easy or as simple as we would like it to be. Truthfully, I would have preferred not to have experienced the bad times just so I could help someone else. However, through these times and my journey I have gained a greater insight and knowledge of God and what it means to be a Christian. I am learning how to tackle the battles I face and how to use God's armour to win them, no longer accepting defeat as my portion, and I honestly hope you will benefit from this also.

Once I committed my life to Christ, all my sins were forgiven and my former ways forgotten by Him. I became that new creature and started my life again with a blank sheet of paper. This is constantly being filled with the knowledge that God has given me through His Words, Grace and Mercy. As I mentioned before the journey hasn't been easy as a Christian, but it has taught me how to deal with the battles I endure in a different way. As you go further into the book and gain an insight into my life, hopefully you will be able to understand what I mean.

How did I get here?

Psalm 139 v 13–15: For You formed my inward parts; You wove me in my mother's womb. I will give thanks to You, for I am fearfully and wonderfully made; Wonderful are Your works, And my soul knows it very well. My frame was not hidden from You, when I was made in secret, and skilfully wrought in the depths of the earth. (NASB – New American Standard Bible)

I was the third child born to West Indian parents in July 1971. My Mother said that she already had a boy and a girl so I was the surprise. Even though I was a surprise to my parents, I definitely was not one to God. My childhood was complicated at times but might be quite similar to many of yours. As I sit here trying to recollect my life and give you an insight into me and my journey, so many thoughts are racing through my mind that I don't know whether to start with the good or the bad.

My first real memories were living in West London with my mum, sister and brother. Mum and dad were separated but dad would come to visit us maybe once or twice a week. I was most definitely a mummy's girl and didn't have much of a relationship with my dad. I don't think he or I really knew where to start. Our home was always filled during the week with family and was always fun. Sometimes we would have sleepovers at one of my aunt's homes and other times have our cousins' stay with us. I was a Seventies baby and there were always children playing outside on our road. I was fairly quiet as a child, but did have a bit of a temper and always wanted to protect my family. Over the years I have come to understand why I acted in this way and hopefully you will be able understand me too.

One example of defending my family was when I discovered that one of dad's brothers had been talking about my Mother criticising the way she had raised us. Mum had always taught us to respect our elders and had raised three children on her own. She also helped to raise her siblings in Barbados along with her nieces and nephews all of whom all have a great deal of respect for her. This uncle was a man who claimed to be a Christian. He was always quoting Scriptures yet lived a very ungodly lifestyle. If asked to give an adjective to best describe him it would be "fake".

I remember him turning up to our home when we were younger wearing a black polo neck jumper and a chain with a large silver cross on it. To be perfectly honest with you his presence often made me shudder and feel extremely uncomfortable. I was in my mid-twenties when I heard what he had said regarding mum. When we came face to face at a family gathering I simply couldn't hold my feelings back and confronted him about it. I defended my mother's honour and told him exactly what I thought. He claimed that he was a God-fearing man, started quoting scriptures and I told him that he hides behind the Bible to cover up his wrongdoings. From that day forward, I could not accept him as family and now call him by his Christian name rather than uncle.

Now if he was an example of a Christian, I would prefer not to have him around. However, I have learnt that God is the final judge and knows your heart; therefore, if he was not being honest and was not living correctly then God would deal with him. Sometimes we don't need to say a word and rise to these things but leave it in God's hands. However, on this occasion I just couldn't help myself, and at that time I wasn't actually a Christian, so that was ok. Wasn't it?

There were other examples, where I would actually be ready to get into physical fights with people in defence of my family. I recall a day I went to the local barber shop after learning that my younger cousin had been attacked by a few boys outside the premises. I believed that the owner didn't do enough to help. I went to the shop on my own, which was pretty full at the time and preceded to give the manager a piece of my mind. That's the kind of person I am, sometimes not thinking about the outcome, but instead charging in to protect my family.

My earliest memories include living in Shepherds Bush in temporary accommodation where we all slept in one bedroom with two beds. We had to share the bathroom and toilet facilities with another family. Mum would never allow us to use the bath. Instead we would use a baby bath in front of the heater in the living room. That is a memory that I will never forget. We weren't rich but our lives were rich in love. Our home was near the local football stadium and it definitely had a community spirit, where children could play freely outside and all the parents knew one another.

When I moved to Fulham at the age of seven into a larger home, mum became a full-time child minder as well as having an evening job at a supermarket. Dad came back to the family home and I started to build a relationship with him. Dad was a British Telecom engineer and every Christmas we would attend his work parties that were held for families. There was always a disco and other activities for the children and we always received amazing presents from Santa. I remember dad taking me out one Sunday to visit some of his friends and family where I was offered food, cake and drinks for the whole day. I was absolutely stuffed but not allowed to refuse anything as Dad said it would be rude. I honestly couldn't eat any more, even though I didn't like some of the things that were being offered I forced myself to consume it as I didn't want to get in trouble. We actually had such a good day and I really believed we were starting to forge a relationship.

One year he took both my sister and brother to Grenada and asked me whether I wanted to go along with them, but as I was a mummy's girl I opted to stay at home. It was really nice just having mum all to myself during the summer holidays. I remember us going to the cinema to see *Superman* and we were able to spend most of the summer holidays without any interruptions. Mum would attend her evening job and whilst she was there my older cousin would collect me and bring me to my aunt's who lived on an estate. I was probably about nine years old and would spend these hours with my younger cousins who were five and one and a half years old at the time.

One evening, my aunty sent me to the shop with my younger cousins. I can't remember what we went to purchase, but I headed off with them in tow, feeling quite grown up. We got to the shop safely, bought what we needed and made our way back. As we were approaching the flats, a man walked towards us asking if we lived around there as he was lost. I asked where he wanted to go and he called the name of the flats we were planning to enter. I told him we were going there and he followed us into the building. Once inside, he suggested we take the stairs and I innocently followed him with my cousins. He said he would offer us some money for a kiss and cuddle. I did feel uncomfortable but didn't want him to touch my younger cousin so I said he could kiss me. He separated me from my cousins and then started to gyrate himself on me. I felt sick and my younger cousin had started to cry and I said I had to go and get him. This stranger then disappeared from the stairwell and we made our way to the lifts to go back to my aunt's. When we told her, she rushed downstairs looking for him, but to no avail, and then the police were called.

Here I was, a nine-year-old trying to tell a policeman what had happened, and even retelling this story in my forties it still sends chills through me. I couldn't sleep properly for ages and didn't want to close my eyes for fear of reliving that day and those images. I am truly thankful that my younger cousin cried as I believe that God was watching over me.

That evening on the way home another auntie collected me. On the walk home she went into pubs and the local McDonalds to see whether he was there. When mum got home from work that evening I was taken to the police station. I listened to mum quite angrily telling the officer on the desk that if she were to find him, she would castrate him and couldn't understand why he didn't go to the West End to find a prostitute rather than prey on a child. That was one of the few times I saw her so angry. Of course, the officer on the desk told her that she should not take the law into her own hands. I honestly don't know what the outcome would have been if he was found, but as I grew older and had my own child I understood those feelings my mum expressed. That a parent would do anything to protect their child. I remember going to school and a child's mother who also lived on the estate heard what had happened and pointed me out to other parents. I overheard them saying, "could it be Jack?" This was a reference to Jack the Ripper who was going around killing ladies of the night in the late 70's early 80's. I just wanted to run away and hide and felt so ashamed. They never found the man, but I pray that he has never done anything like that or worse to any other child.

I was also bullied by a neighbour from the age of five until we moved to a new home. This girl was the same age as I was and was meant to be my friend, but would often make me do things that I wasn't comfortable with, such as doing little sexual acts with her in the guttering of her home. I was too scared to tell my mum or anyone else for fear of getting into trouble. I didn't know what else to do but follow her orders. I really thought that I was to blame, but as the years went on I realised that she must have had issues at home that made her behave in such a way.

There was one time during a school play when I was given the leading role as Sleeping Beauty and she was the witch. She wasn't satisfied with that part in the play and wanted to be Sleeping Beauty. I was ordered by her that I should inform the teacher that I didn't want to do it. I went to the teacher and told her just that. But she said that it was my role and it was too late to change it. When I went back to tell my so called 'friend' that the teacher wouldn't let me change places, I was told by this evil child to make it happen. So, I went back to the teacher and cried my little heart out until she gave in. I was then playing the part that I didn't want to play just to make someone else happy because I was afraid to speak up. This was pretty much the story for most of my life.

As years went on, somehow, I couldn't stop thinking that I deserved to be abused and mistreated. But at the same time, I was strong enough and willing to put myself on the line to protect my family and the people I cared for as I didn't want them to suffer.

As my story unravels you will get a better picture, but only God knows why He allowed me to go through these experiences.

Part 1

Struggling

Chapter 1

The Power of God's Might

How many times have you heard people say "God is good"? Well I can agree that he really is good. All of the time!

Isaiah 54 v 7–8 – For a small moment have I forsaken thee but with great mercies I will gather thee. In a little wrath I hid my face from thee for a moment but with everlasting kindness will I have mercy on thee saith the Lord thy Redeemer. (KJV – King James Version)

We are God's children, and just like any parent whose child may disappoint them we are there to teach them a life lesson. We may turn away from them for a while, maybe to help that child fend for themselves and gain a level of maturity/wisdom. Eventually that parent will check in on their child to see how they are getting on and continue to help them on their way. The love is unconditional. Nothing can break the bond between parent and child and you will show mercy upon the child and forgive them for their misdemeanours. That is the kind of love God has for us and we are connected through an invisible umbilical cord which is the spirit that lives within us giving us a direct link to the Father.

This chapter is to prove just how powerful God is and is just an example of His capabilities. Very often people believe that they can get through situations without any support or assistance. However, that is so far from the truth. God can move mountains, the obstacles which we are unable to move that prevent you from doing His work. He is a mighty and powerful God. He is God Almighty!

He is the leader, physician, comforter, provider, protector, amongst many other things. A God with no limitations. The all-seeing and all-knowing God. He knows what you will do before you even do it; nothing is a secret to Him. God knows your heart and lives within you.

He shows you grace and mercy and allows you to rise today. So, you should be thankful.

My experiences below identified my need for God. By relying upon Him and seeking Him through fervent prayer and having others intervening for me, He was able to show Himself mightily in my life.

I have seen the Father work through me over the years, even when I thought I wasn't worthy of His time. In the spring of 2012, He moved me in a way that I could never have imagined. It wasn't a particularly good time for me. I was suffering from depression, deep in the pit of despair and didn't know how to rise up from it. Church or people simply weren't cutting it for me. I was just going through the motions, existing but not living. The beginning of the year had been very challenging for me to say the least with so many twists and turns, but throughout it God had been on my side. I was totally burnt out and was signed off work for two months. During that period I sought counselling which was really painful for me. There was a heavy and dark cloud looming over me which prevented me from having any clear direction, vision or belief in myself. I was totally lost and in desperate need of joy and peace. I struggled with my thoughts and was feeling so negative, but understood that God was cleansing and healing me from my past. He wanted me to move forward so that I could make a commitment to Him.

I spoke to my Pastor about how I felt and she encouraged me to not give up and prayed for me. But even that made no difference to the way I felt. For many years I had been encouraged by others to get baptised. I can be quite strong-willed at times and therefore won't be forced into something if I don't agree with it. I also believe that nothing happens before the time and needed to be fully committed, otherwise there would be no point. In 2012, I believed God was calling me to do this and I advised the Pastor that I was ready and I wanted to be more committed to the Lord.

From then on things started to change. I gradually went back to church, started to attend Bible and baptism classes and God commenced His work in me. I began to speak in tongues, delivered messages to people and He was constantly giving me new songs, even having me dancing at church services as well as healing me from the inside. I was being used in praise and worship to affect others' lives. I am not trying to glorify myself or overestimate my capabilities as I know that God deserves all the glory and it was Him working through me. I just allowed myself to decrease so that He could increase. I know for a fact that He was present at that time as I would never have got up and danced, especially in front of an audience. The only time I would dance is at a party or in the club, but He ordered me to do so and I chose to be obedient to Him. God will take you out of your comfort zone when you least expect it. That's the power of God's might!

Within that period of time, He also delivered me out of my depression and gave me the joy, peace and strength that I needed to continue on my journey. My GP had offered me tablets to help with the depression, which I went and purchased. I even told God that was not my portion and He needed to fix me, as I couldn't get any lower than this. Thankfully, I didn't take the tablets but God did fix me over a period of time. He obviously saw that I could not take any more and gave me the medicine that I needed, which was more of Him. It was most definitely a humbling experience and I could see things a lot more clearly. The following lyrics from the song *Amazing Grace* finally resonated with me:

"I once was lost, but now am found, was blind but now I see". Just as Saul was blinded on the road to Damascus and his eyes were opened when he reached his destination, my eyes were opened also.

I had a new lease on life and when it came to the day of my baptism I was truly ready and free. It was a pivotal moment in my life and an amazing day as my daughter had also decided to get baptised. There was also an additional baptism on the day, so as much as I believed that God had planned that day for me, I realised He had a bigger plan. Strangely enough, that person also attended the Baptism classes having recently been saved but said she was not ready to be baptised. I told her that I could see it happening and she had better bring some white clothes along on the day. She didn't but God had already prepared the clothing for her without her knowledge. He is awesome!

God had also used me in awesome ways even when I felt I was unworthy. I would be woken at seemingly unreasonable and irregular hours of the morning to send messages of encouragement to people, even though I didn't know what the messages meant. Those people came back to me confirming that the words were exactly what they needed and God was responding to their prayers. I am so glad that I was obedient, even if somewhat tired. But being used as a vessel for Christ really encouraged and lifted me up during that period.

I have also been given warnings through dreams and one in particular really helped me to deal with a situation on a different level when I was confronted with it. The dream showed me in a room with a new boss and we were having a meeting. I didn't know what it related to but I started to get very angry with her, giving her a piece of my mind. Strong language was used by me to get my point across before I finally stormed out of the room. I didn't pay too much attention to the dream after that. However, at that time I was on a secondment at work where I should have been receiving higher duty pay for the role I was undertaking. My current line manager was trying her best to ensure I received it but the head of the department, who I had already clashed with, kept creating obstacles and delays, so a meeting was called at short notice. I was due to work directly for this lady as a personal assistant following a reorganisation, and the first time I met her my spirit didn't take to her. She had a very controlling nature and was quite rude too. I declared on that day that I would never work for her and God created the opportunity for the secondment to take place. All I wanted was what was rightfully mine and to be paid for the job I was undertaking as Programme Manager.

The meeting commenced and I explained the situation and that I had already been performing the role for six months. She was aware of this and I had asked that any pay should be backdated to that date. I was then told by her that this couldn't be done as it would create a black hole in HR. All I thought was it would actually show her incompetence as a manager. When I questioned her about it, she made a remark which implied that I had an attitude, then threatened to put me back in my substantive post. At that moment the dream came immediately to my memory. I knew it was an attack of the enemy; he wanted me to start screaming and cursing in the hope that I would lose my job. So I calmly told her that I wasn't happy with her trying to defame my character and she could do what she wanted. We then closed the meeting but admittedly I left there fuming. When I saw my mother in the evening I ran through the story and told her, "This woman thinks she's in control, but God is in control".

The following day I went to work feeling light and carefree when I was approached by this same woman. Her attitude had changed and she appeared very humble, promising that she would get the higher duty pay sorted as a matter of urgency. This was finally done and the day it was approved she couldn't wait to come and let me know. The secondment ended and I was given a new role following a restructure and never worked for this lady just as I had declared. How powerful is my God?

It is only when I moved closer to Him and searched for Him through necessity that he revealed Himself to me letting me know that He is with me at all times. By opening up yourself to God, He will prove Himself in such a powerful way, giving you the strength to move those stumbling blocks that are preventing you from moving forward.

Even though we are weathering a storm and feel as if we don't want to continue, God will calm that storm. We just need to rely on Him to take charge of the helm and carry us through the rough seas, bringing us to a safe place where the waters are calm.

The Bible shows you the many ways you can tap into God's power. Listed below are a few Scriptures that I hold onto as a reminder:

Psalm 40 v 1–3 - I waited patiently for the Lord and He inclined unto me, and heard my cry. He brought me up also out of a horrible pit, out of the miry clay and set my feet upon a rock and established my goings. And He hath put a new song in my mouth, even praise unto our God; many shall see it, and fear and shall trust in the Lord. (KJV)

Matthew 6 v 33 – But seek ye first the kingdom of God and His righteousness and all these things shall be added onto you. (KJV)

Proverbs 3 v 5–6 – Trust in the Lord with all thine heart and lean not unto thine own understanding; in all thy ways acknowledge Him and He shall direct your paths. (KJV)

Exodus 14v4 – The Lord shall fight for you and ye shall hold your peace. (KJV)

Psalm 91 v 1 – He that dwelleth in the secret place of the most High shall abide under the shadow of the Almighty. (KJV)

Chapter 2

Feelings

Ask yourself the following questions:

- How am I feeling?
- What do I go to church to feel?
- Do I go to feel the presence of God, to be part of a family or to feel freedom?

I have had to ask myself if we are honest as Christians as to how we feel. We believe that we should always give the same answer when people ask us how we are doing. Such as, "Well God is good" or "I am holding on by God's grace". Sometimes you can see that the person is in pain and not being completely honest but they are just putting up a façade. What do we actually do to help them to heal? We are constantly performing and living far from genuine lives, not only as Christians. I believe most of us are playing a part that we want others to see. However, when we are by ourselves and the mask is removed, who we really are is revealed. Who are you covering up? Where is the real you? Where is that genuine person who craves approval and validation? You will never get that if you cannot allow your true self to be known, not only by your friends and peers, but by God Himself. Although He always knows our true nature, you cannot reveal your desire to Him if you cannot allow yourself to express it.

Don't get me wrong; we know God is good and I would never say anything different because He has kept me to this day and blessed me in so many ways. I believe that sharing our feelings with others and being honest can not only help us, but can help others who may be experiencing the same trials. Remember we are not alone and we can encourage and comfort one another throughout these situations. No man is an island! We are not unique unto ourselves when it comes to the need for blessings, feeling hurt or depressed, and going through difficult trials.

When going through trials or even triumphs, human beings experience a mixture of emotions such as anger, resentment, jealousy, bitterness, confusion, joy, happiness, peace, and exhilaration. Emotion is part of the human experience. When they are positive that's great! But what do we do when they are the opposite? We are told that we should ignore them and should not live our lives based on feelings. However, they can be so overwhelming sometimes that it is impossible to ignore them. We were not given emotions so they should be ignored. The trick is to not be controlled by them. Ignoring your emotions can make these feelings/emotions spiral out of control leading us into a pit of despair where we struggle to get out of the funk. We then get more vexed because we're vexed, more frustrated because we're frustrated, and so on. These feelings could have emanated through experiencing a loss of something or someone, and we feel grieved. Your children may be playing up and you don't know what to do. A partner or loved one does something hurtful towards you and you just can't find it in yourself to forgive them. A situation at work could be getting you down and you don't know how to solve it. You could be a single parent raising your child with no help. Unemployed or even employed and struggling to make ends meet, wondering where the next set of money is coming from. Literally robbing Peter to pay Paul. Things from the past coming back to haunt you! You may have suffered abuse, verbally or physically, as a child. Felt neglected by parents, family or friends. Your mother or father may have been absent which has created low self-esteem, depression or anxiety. You then wonder 'why me?' and throw yourself the biggest pity party. These feelings can become deep rooted. Therefore we will need to go deep underground to uproot them before we can move on and become what God wants us to be. This is only possible if we decide to let go.

Remember, we are all human but things may impact us in different ways because of our past experiences and even our upbringing. What might seem like a major issue to one person might not affect another in the same way. Our coping mechanisms can be quite different. Something may not bother one person, whilst others may be overwhelmed by the same situation. And these differences may show up even within the same family.

You may believe that seeking alternative solutions can help you cope with these situations; chocolate, comfort eating, spending sprees, alcohol, drugs, sex, or self-harming. I have tried some of these methods and know people who have also chosen some of these alternatives, so believe me when I say you will find they are only temporary fixes and do not provide a solution. They will only exacerbate the problem and bring you deeper into that pit because they do not address the root cause.

I don't know about you, but when I first got saved, I thought it was all clear sailing from there. I felt that nothing could get to me and left church with an inner peace and joy, wanting to declare from the top of the mountain that my feet were firmly set upon, how happy I was to have accepted God into my life. When I told my partner that I had been saved, the first thing he asked was, "Where does that leave me?" I simply said it was not about him but about my relationship with God. It may have sounded a little selfish, but this was about my salvation and did not involve anyone else. It almost seemed as if he was jealous of God. But my relationship with God was separate to the one I had with him. Someone mentioned to me that being a Christian was hard, but I believed I could handle it. I felt like Xena the Warrior Princess ready to take on anything or anyone. How naïve I was. My salvation was when the real tests and trials started to come. My relationship broke down with my daughter's father. I had struggles at work and my finances were dire. I started to experience health issues and these things became so overwhelming and challenging that I started to descend that mountain at great speed. Even through my struggles I constantly searched for that same feeling I had had when I first got saved. I yearned for it through necessity, the feeling of being filled with joy, peace, faith, hope, and experiencing an unconditional love. I have reached a place where I didn't think I could have fallen any deeper, but I remembered to call on the Lord for Him to deliver me out of my distresses.

Through these trials and over the years I have learnt that in the midst of throwing my pity parties, I should still continue to find comfort in God's word and have faith. Sometimes things can turn around suddenly and everyone is happy to have this quick fix. Yet other times we may need to dwell in that place for a while.

You might ask yourself why you should have to endure this burden for so long. I have listed below a few reasons why these delays may occur:

1. We need to experience these things so that when we come out on the other side we can recognise God's mercy and give Him the glory.
2. We can look back and see where God has taken us from and have faith He is bringing us to a better place.
3. God may want us to learn a lesson through these times. He may reveal things to us that we were not aware of, in particular where we may have unforgiveness in our hearts or may have sinned in another way.
4. We need to understand why we are feeling these things. As painful as it is going through it, we can learn something valuable about ourselves and deal with these issues. Oftentimes we tend to ignore them and they may come back to bite us.
5. Once they are dealt with we can eventually release the burden and no longer be held captive by it.
6. God wants us to rely on Him to see us through.
7. He wants to see how faithful we are to Him.

I believe we need to feel and be in touch with our emotions and also empathise with others who are going through situations, even if we don't understand them. We cannot be emotionless, not as Christians. Jesus felt inclined to help many people no matter what he was feeling.

Therefore, throughout our situations we still need to be able to support and encourage others. Sometimes it's hard to encourage people whilst feeling discouraged yourself.

Do you sometimes ask the question, "If I am saved then why should I have to suffer?" I believe that the following scripture provides the answer.

1 Peter 5 v 10 – And after you have suffered a little while, the God of all grace (who imparts all blessing and favour) who has called you into His (own) eternal glory in Christ, will Himself complete and make you what you ought to be, establish and ground you securely and strengthen and settle you. (AMP – Amplified)

It says that although we feel all of these negative emotions they are temporary. Therefore, we should not lose faith that God is there because He will ground and settle us making us what we ought to be. By facing adversity, it builds up resilience, strength and character within us.

He knows your every thought and hears you when you cry out in pain. No parent wants to see their child suffering and will come to their rescue to help ease their pain, but they cannot do anything unless you cry out to them. So, you shouldn't have to suffer in silence. Any child of West Indian parentage will definitely remember their parents making the statement, "If you don't hear, you will feel". That is basically saying I have warned you about this on numerous occasions and if you don't want to listen then eventually you will feel the consequences of your actions. However, as parents, we can only do so much, and if your child continues to do the same thing after you have told them not to, their behaviour may eventually disappoint you. Some of us may turn away from them for a while or even scold them to teach that child a lesson or to allow them to fend for themselves and gain a level of maturity.

Isaiah 43 v 1 When you pass through the waters, I will be with you, and through the rivers, they will not overwhelm you. When you walk through the fire, you will not be burned or scorched, nor will the flame kindle upon you. (AMP)

In the Bible, God's children, Jeremiah, David, Daniel and Job amongst many others, endured many difficulties throughout their lives and they weren't always filled with joy. Sometimes they felt forsaken by God and could not feel the presence of this Lord that they served. They felt trapped in the wilderness all alone, but when they cried to the Lord in their despair He brought them out of their circumstances. We are not the first to go through these situations and we won't be the last. Isaiah 43 V 1 tells us that God is with us through all of our circumstances.

Remember the Lord can do all things. He can also create the situations as a test of our faith. It is not always the devil's work.

Psalm 107 v 25 31 – For He commands and raises up the stormy wind, which lifts up the waves of the sea. [Those aboard] mount up to the heavens, they go down again to the deeps; their courage melts away because of their plight. They reel to and fro and stagger like a drunken man and are at their wits' end [all their wisdom has come to nothing]. Then they cry to the Lord in their trouble, and He brings them out of their distresses. He hushes the storm to a calm and to a gentle whisper, so that the waves of the sea are still. Then the men are glad because of the calm, and He brings them to their desired haven. Oh, that men would praise [and confess to] the Lord for His goodness and loving-kindness and His wonderful works to the children of men! (AMP)

As Christians we may have to endure these situations and tests at times, but remember it is only for a time. So, hold fast in God, standing on His word throughout, believing and having faith that He can calm those storms and raise us up out of the pit.

Now what is faith? We have heard these words quoted many times on our journey from *Hebrews 11 v 1: Now faith is the assurance (the confirmation, the title deed) of the things [we] hope for, being the proof of things [we] do not see and the conviction of their reality [faith perceiving as real fact what is not revealed to the senses]. (AMP)*

Further in Hebrews 11, it also highlights a number of people who were prompted by faith, such as Noah who was forewarned about the floods and built an ark on faith. Abraham was willing to sacrifice his only son and went onto a place obeying God, not knowing that God already had a ram as a sacrifice in the place of Abraham's son, Isaac. There was also Sarah who conceived a child at such a late stage in her life, and the list goes on.

As mentioned earlier, throughout these trials there may be revelations about ourselves and our behaviours that need to be addressed. As Christians, we are not perfect, but each time we go through a situation it can teach us patience, humility and selflessness. It can also bring us closer to perfection and most importantly help us to establish a closer relationship with God. So, we need to accept these feelings, deal with them, release them and move forward never forgetting that God has forgiven us of our sins and we need to learn to forgive ourselves.

We should, however, seek repentance for our sins and any unforgiveness we are carrying in our hearts. Jealousy, hate, lust, and anger are all sins. It's difficult to show love or forgiveness towards someone that might have offended you in some way. It is an even greater job for God to show us love and forgiveness when we offend Him every day, yet He does.

At given times throughout the year we are asked by the church to fast. I am certain that we have all carried out individual fasts. Fasting is almost like a detox. A cleansing of the spirit. A removal of all the impurities that are clogging our hearts and minds preventing us from getting closer to God. Fasting and praying are opportunities for God to reveal to us where we are falling short. Highlighting where there is any unforgiveness in our hearts. Revealing to us areas where we might have offended someone by our attitude and need to seek their forgiveness. Some people wait until the New Year to make changes in their lives and see it as a time for discarding the things of old. Clothes for example may become a little bit tighter after eating too much, restricting our movement. We may then make a resolution to go on a diet, so that our clothes will fit better allowing us to feel more comfortable. Just like the physical things we are carrying, our emotional baggage may be restricting our movement and progress, preventing us from stepping into a more comfortable environment. We shouldn't be governed by our past. Instead we should allow ourselves to move forward into the present with faith and hope knowing that God has a better plan for us. We cannot reach that place if we allow our feelings to weigh us down.

I believe it is ok to feel, but that we should not dwell upon these emotions. We must recognise that God has brought us through many trials and He will see us through the next ones. We will have the victory. Remember to have faith. But when you do feel these things be honest with yourself and dig deep. Ask God to give you insight and understanding and reveal to you where there is unforgiveness or sin. You might not like what is revealed but will need to accept it to enable you to move on. Once it is identified it will need to be uprooted, discarded and new seeds planted. Seeds of forgiveness, faith, hope, and love which will allow you to flourish, grow and spread your branches. Not to wither away so that people will not want to eat from us. Do not forget that your behaviours and feelings can have a negative impact on others around you.

Following a teaching I led on Christians being slaves, which is later mentioned in the book, I opened this up for discussion. Some of the members felt that Christians are still living in bondage and that we alone are responsible for keeping ourselves in that position. If this is true for you, unless you are willing to look deeper into your behaviours, you will continue to be bound and not live a life of freedom that God has promised to you.

Ask yourself today, "Is there any unforgiveness in me? Have I offended anyone?" Ask God to reveal this to you through fasting and prayer. Ask Him to help you understand these feelings and enable you to manage them without letting them overwhelm you. Ask that He help you to put them under subjection.

We all know about the seasons and how they change, which are similar to our feelings and experiences in that they only last for a time. With some of the freak weather we have experienced in the UK over the years, it is not impossible to get snow in the springtime. This tells us that we need to be prepared for the unexpected. Some of us aren't able to put our winter clothing away until at least the end of June and wellies are always kept close to hand. I very rarely leave home without an umbrella in my bag as the weather can be unpredictable. Therefore we should always be prepared for adverse conditions. If we begin to meditate upon the word of God we can overcome these adversities.

God knows exactly how you are feeling and is in control.

Daniel 2 v 21-22 He changes the times and the seasons, He removes kings and sets up kings. He gives wisdom to the wise and knowledge to those who have understanding. He reveals the deep and secret things. He knows what is in the darkness and the light dwells within Him. (AMP)

I believe that we can overcome these feelings if we remember the following:

1. We are overcomers! *Revelation 12 v 11 And they overcame Him by the blood of the lamb and by the word of their testimony they did not love their lives to the death. (NKJV)*

2. We serve a mighty and powerful God – The doctor might have prescribed all kinds of tablets that they believe can get you out of your situation. But ask God to heal and restore you for He is the ultimate healer/physician.

3. The battle is not yours, but God's. You are not fighting this by yourself, just pass all of your cares and concerns over to Him.

4. We are not victims but victors – You are clothed with God's armour and no weapon formed against you shall prosper.

Chapter 3

Brokenness

Psalm 31 v 7–12 – I will be glad and rejoice in your mercy and steadfast love, because you have seen my affliction, you have taken note of my life's distresses. And you have not given me into the hand of the enemy; you have set my feet in a broad place. Have mercy and be gracious unto me, O Lord, for I am in trouble; with grief my eye is weakened, also my inner self and my body. For my life is spent with sorrow and my years with sighing; my strength has failed because of my iniquity, and even my bones have wasted away. To all my enemies I have become a reproach, but especially to my neighbours, and a dread to my acquaintances, who flee from me on the street. I am forgotten like a dead man, and out of mind; like a broken vessel am I. (AMP)

Have you ever felt broken to the point of despair? Having nowhere to run and no-one to meet you at the point of your needs. No one to console you, comfort or protect you and you are feeling totally alone?

Life can become overwhelming and everyday situations can lead us to become depressed, stressed, anxious, bitter, angry and for some people even suicidal. When you are at that place what do you do? We tend to give up as nothing we do or try seems to work or makes us feel better. If it does work the repair is only temporary and we start to crack under the pressure of keeping up the façade until eventually we are broken into pieces. You may have reached the depths of despair, where nobody can help you. Believe me I've been there, feeling broken, emotionally, mentally and physically. Someone may come along and pick up some of the pieces, but because we may be so damaged, they as well as ourselves, don't quite know where that piece fits or even if it belongs anymore.

In the **Chapter 'The Power of God's Might',** I mention that in 2012 I was going through a very low period which went on for some months. I was feeling desperate, lost sight of who I was, had no direction, and was extremely emotional. I was definitely not a pleasure to be around and therefore started to withdraw from people. Nothing seemed to help and church didn't feel like the right place for me. I couldn't face work, didn't want to talk and felt totally disengaged from everything. I was numb! I know that family and friends were praying for me and they were very concerned for my wellbeing.

One day I received a call from a friend and our conversations would normally have been filled with laughter. However, on this occasion, I was totally zoned out and couldn't register anything she was saying. I ended the conversation and even though I could hear the concern in her voice, I honestly didn't have anything to say. Nothing could get me out of my stink. I had hit rock bottom and was purely existing, running on autopilot. Throughout this time I still had to continue to care for my ten-year-old, catering to all her needs when I was barely able to care for myself. I cried so hard and thought I was losing the plot. This was pretty much how things were for me at the time. Tears were constantly flowing and one day I was lying on my bedroom floor in a heap saying to myself that I can't get any lower than this. I wanted tears of joy and not pain.

A colleague/friend of mine was going on a prayer weekend with her church and asked me on the Friday what I wanted her to pray for. I asked her to pray for joy and peace for me and that once I received that, then everything else should fall into place. I just wanted to get out of the pit, however, could not find a way out no matter what I tried. Being in a total state of despair, first thing Monday morning I managed to find her and asked if she had prayed for me as I still felt the same. All she said was, "It is done", so I held onto those words. I had also visited the doctor who stated that I was suffering from depression and prescribed me Diazepam. I refused to accept that was my portion and during that week I spoke to God. Admittedly I was very harsh as I was feeling so desperate at that point. It was as if I was challenging Him and needed Him to prove Himself to me. My exact words were, "I am telling everyone you are the healer and you are my drug, so fix me!"

My breakthrough came in a matter of days and He met the challenge when I least expected it. I was just on my knees at home praying for others, not even thinking about myself or my current situation. All of a sudden I felt a stirring in my spirit and God started to do a work in me. I started praying in tongues, not even knowing what was going on, but I put my total trust in Him.

I was laid out on the floor when my deliverance took place. It was like I was having an outer body experience where I was looking down on myself from above and could see the old me being removed and I was being transformed. When I looked in the mirror there was such an apparent change in my appearance. I kept looking deeper in the mirror and could see and feel God within me. I recognised myself again, the Karen that had been hidden for so long, but was now filled with joy, inner peace and a clearer vision. Which was all that I had been praying for. When others saw me, they couldn't believe the transformation. God truly is an effective drug. I was on such a high and called my mum straight away. I was running around my flat like a lunatic as I was no longer bound and felt like I could continue running for miles. The burdens and heaviness had been removed and that day, as I collected my daughter from school, the first thing she said was, "Mummy, you look different". I began to walk with my head held high and had a light surrounding me which seemed to cause people to draw closer to me. I was like the child in the Ready Brek adverts that would have a glow surrounding him after eating his cereal.

God *can* step in at any time, but he will *always* step in if we invite Him in to repair and restore us. And this may not happen in the way that we want or expect. Sometimes the work in you will be anything but what you want, but it will always be done for a reason.

For years, the world has been encouraging us to recycle to save the environment, but this is not a new thing. God has been recycling His children for thousands of years. In the past, we would discard all of our rubbish in one place, but now most people will separate it. We now put the things that are sustainable into different bags according to its intended purpose. Once recycled, it may have a totally different purpose than the one it originally started with. That's what God does with us. He takes the good bits and discards of the unusable stuff, things that aren't important or things that may add some value to us as His children, and gives those bits – and us – a new purpose.

Thinking about this, I then began to wonder about how glass was made and the process that takes place to create such a delicate yet strong object and how it is moulded by the glassmaker to form a perfect glass. In particular, a recycled glass that had been damaged or broken in pieces that is beyond repair. I started to imagine myself being that glass and would like you to do the same.

Imagine you are a glass with lots of cracks or even a glass that was chipped. You might still be able to drink from it but it may cut the person who is using it. They may not want to use it again for fear of being hurt so might even put it away out of sight or simply discard of it. If you were the owner of this glass, what would you do with it? If you, the glass, were continually used, that chip may eventually get bigger with constant washing, banging and possibly being dropped along the way. Inevitably, that chip would become a crack and the liquid would start to seep out and be of no use to anyone. What choice would the owner have but to discard of this glass? They could try to repair it but it will still have cracks and chips with little pieces missing or pieces that can't be reused. It just wouldn't fit perfectly. But God can remove those pieces that do not fit perfectly. If the glass were thrown into the bin with other rubbish it would be crushed further, hidden away never to be seen again. But put into the correct recycling bag the glass can be separated and distributed to the correct place to be recycled.

When glass is being recycled it will be crushed down further, ground down and put through intense heat to melt it down. Which is what it feels like when we are going through the extreme pressure we feel in our most dire situations. I know that's how I felt at my lowest moment.

Glass originates from sand, flint (rock) and spar. The materials for making glass must be reduced to powder. Just as man was created from dust. After sifting out the coarse parts, proper proportions of silex (ground stone) and flux are mixed together and put into a furnace kept in a moderate heat for a number of hours. The silex is frequently stirred during the process. The matter it produces is called frit, which is then easily converted into glass by pounding and vitrifying in melting pots of the glass furnace. Making fine glass will sometimes require a small addition of flux to the frit to correct any fault. As the flux is the most expensive article, the manufacturer will rather put too little at first as he can always remedy this defect in the melting pot. God will give us just the right measure of what we need and keep adding to us as and when necessary. The heat in the furnace must be kept up until the glass is brought to a state of perfect fusion and during this process any scum which arises must be removed by ladles. When the glass is perfectly melted the glassblowers commence their operations.

God is the glassblower and will commence His operation molding and shaping us into the perfect glass with no imperfections. We may have started off as a beer glass or bottle, used and abused by many people. But He has restored us into a fine piece of glass where only the best wine can be poured into and served. That wine is the spirit of God, the living water that everyone will want to drink from.

What should you do in these broken times? I advise you to continue serving God and humble yourself knowing that in due time He will exalt you.

Isaiah 41 v 9–10 reads: You whom I [the Lord] have taken from the ends of the earth and have called from the corners of it, and said to you, You are My servant – I have chosen you and not cast you off [even though you are exiled]. Fear not [there is nothing to fear], for I am with you; do not look around you in terror and be dismayed, for I am your God. I will strengthen and harden you to difficulties, yes, I will help you; yes, I will hold you up and retain you with my [victorious] right hand of rightness and justice. (AMP)

This scripture says that we need to serve God at all times, we have been chosen by Him and we are therefore precious in His sight. Although we may feel abandoned (in exile) and a lost cause, God has not cast us away. So therefore, we should be fully reliant on Him to take us out of the dark places. Don't look around in terror and allow the place you are in to overwhelm you, as God will give you the strength to continue and will lead you to the other side.

Matthew 6 v 25–27 says that we should not be anxious for anything. The Lord has fed the birds and we are more valuable than they. By worrying it will not add a single hour to our lives, but prevents us from living our lives to the full.

We all know that life is not easy and we all face different challenges every day, some that can make us or even break us. Therefore, I would like you to remember these words when you are feeling broken!

I am a vessel for Christ; although I may be broken God will repair me. I will carry His word and am filled with the Holy Spirit.

Do not forget that you are strong and can overcome any situation, trial or obstacle. The Lord is our strength which means that we have been given supernatural power.

Remember that you are valued by God and although at times you may feel broken you are not beyond repair as God is the restorer of all things. Ask Him to restore you back to your former glory.

Chapter 4

Finding Strength

Jeremiah 1 v 5 Before I formed you in the womb I knew you, before you were born I set you apart; I appointed you as a prophet to the nations. (NIV)

Jeremiah 1 v 17 Get yourself ready! Stand up and say to them whatever I command you. Do not be terrified by them, or I will terrify you before them. (NIV)

As a child, I was very much into reading and would often volunteer to read out loud or was often encouraged by the teachers to do so. This really helped with my confidence as I was very shy but it was something that I felt very comfortable doing when asked. When I started secondary school, I remember volunteering to read in an English lesson. I stood up and started to read but could hear talking and sniggering from the back of the classroom by two girls, one who I believed to be my friend. I could feel myself get really hot and flustered and wished the room would swallow me up, but I managed to finish reading the text and sat down feeling really discouraged. That day had such a major impact on my confidence that I never volunteered to read again. In fact, they may not have actually been talking or laughing at me, but I couldn't see any other reason as to why it couldn't be me. I then became so fearful of speaking out in front of people because I thought the response would be the same. Oftentimes I would begin to run many scenarios through my mind to eventually talk myself out of doing it.

As years went by, some of my work roles would require me to speak in front of people. I would have to run training sessions and assessment centres but I honestly didn't feel confident doing it. Eventually I attended a presentation skills course at work where the attendees were asked to produce a presentation on a topic of their choosing to present in front of the class. This presentation was also to be recorded at the time. When it was my turn, I started to speak with a confident flow, then a panic overcame me. I thought I wasn't making any sense and could feel these eyes staring back at me. I then blurted out during my presentation 'I can't do this' but was encouraged by the rest of the group that I could and so I continued. When I reviewed the recording after, I actually did very well, but it was my mind and self-perception and probably the fear from childhood that made me freeze.

I eventually got a job as a Programme Manager and was asked to speak in front of a group of 60 people. I had now received my training and my boss wanted to take me out of my comfort zone. Opportunities were given to me to speak at church before, but those tended to be in front of people I knew and I was speaking from the heart and sharing my experience. However, this was a little different as here I was having to sell a product and remain professional. When I stood up and saw the audience's faces I literally wanted to run out of the room. Silently I prayed to God asking Him to help me and give me the courage. I finally delivered my presentation and as soon as it was over, I darted out of the room literally shaking. One of my colleagues who attended provided me with feedback. She said that initially I looked scared but my confidence grew as I went on. I have managed to present since then but not without preparing and knowing my subject.

I was then driven to run a workshop at church called *The Art of Public Speaking and Presenting*. Christians are meant to be representatives of Christ and should be prepared to speak at all times, so I believed it was something that God wanted me to do. Having looked around the church, I felt that there were so many members that were not reaching their full potential. I believed they had a bigger role to play within the church, but were not given the opportunity or did not feel confident enough to speak up. I wanted them to step out of their comfort zone just as I had done as I believed the purpose that God had for their lives was not being met. Managing to get approval from the pastor, I ran a few workshops for the church members. I soon discovered that the shy people were quietly confident and the ones that were bold in church were actually quite shy when it came to presenting. Even my mum, sister and daughter attended and they were all awesome. It taught the participants that if they have confidence in their subject matter, then even if they messed up the audience would not be aware. Therefore they needed to change the perception of self. I even shared my childhood experience which none of them could have imagined me going through because I was confident in the subject I was teaching. By running this course and speaking publicly, I found strength in what I thought people perceived as a weakness in me and turned it around. I pray that I will be given an opportunity to run further workshops for less confident people and those suffering from low self-esteem and believe that both teenagers and adults will definitely benefit from them.

As well as struggling in finding strength and courage in the example given above there were many other experiences that I have had to endure in my life where I have had to fight through and overcome. Another example is when I discovered my ex-partner was cheating on me and I felt completely broken. I had my suspicions and mentioned it to him, but he told me that I was being paranoid. Our relationship was flowing fairly well or maybe that's what I wanted to believe. Why would it be to the contrary when we had a beautiful little girl, which to me was the perfect family setting? Why on Earth would anyone want to jeopardise that? Although we didn't live together, we would spend a lot of time doing things as a family unit. My sixth sense or instinct kicked in and my spirit just didn't feel right. Maybe this was because I had similar experiences with previous partners. My Poirot senses kicked in and I started to investigate further. Sad to say I started to snoop, looking for evidence to confirm my suspicions. They say if you keep looking you will eventually find what you are looking for. I would check his phone and even gained access to his email account which almost became habitual. What a crazy time it was. But his behaviour had changed and this didn't sit right with me. He worked shifts and as a surprise on his birthday I drove to his work place, baby in tow to give him his birthday card and present. I remember him being so happy to see us and he said he didn't want us to go. The next day I undertook my habitual check and discovered email exchanges between him and the lady he was cheating on me with. In the email I had also found he had been to see her after he finished work on his birthday. When I read the message I was at work at the time and sat at my desk in total shock. I had gone in search of this and here was the evidence right in front of me. I emailed them both to let them know I was aware of what was going on. He was in shock and I was in pain. How could he do this to me? Deceive me and damage our family? It was too much to bear but I carried on not mentioning it to any of my family or friends and just worked through the pain for years. We tried to patch things up but over the years I could see that it wasn't working. My trust had been betrayed.

Many evenings I used to stand at the window staring at the sky, thinking 'this isn't working', but immediately dismissed the thoughts. Maybe I was fearful of being alone, being a single parent and being seen as a failure by not being able to keep a man. I don't know if I was expecting an answer from God and the heavens to answer me but I tried everything to keep it together, arranging little breaks, nights out as well as trying to spend more quality time together, but nothing worked. There was no peace and I just couldn't let go or heal. Then the inevitable day came when I told him it wasn't working. He also agreed and unfortunately, we separated when our daughter was five years old. Throughout our relationship, we had talked about moving in together and his parents and my mum were so keen for us to get married. He even told my mum that he would. So why was this all going wrong? Everyone loved him, but the love had gone from the relationship between us. I then had to take the route I didn't want and become a single mother, raising my daughter by myself. I felt that I had invested so much into him and he threw it away so easily.

I eventually found the courage to step away from the relationship that wasn't bringing me any joy or peace. Over the years, I did go through a major grieving process for the loss of this relationship. You may ask why it took me so long, but everyone moves through things at different paces. I stood on the side lines and watched him getting on with his life. He was also introducing our child to other women he had started new relationships with, which was extremely painful for me at times. I had to experience the following five stages of grief before I could move on:

Stage 1 – Denial

Stage 2 – Anger

Stage 3 – Bargaining

Stage 4 – Depression

Stage 5 – Acceptance

These stages were initially categorised in a study of those who had lost a loved one, but they can be applied to any type of major loss. Not only do we grieve when a loved one passes, it can happen with the loss of a job or the breakup of a relationship, even if two people are not married. And in my case, it was the break up with my daughter's father. I also went through this cycle when I discovered I had diabetes and my stages of grief have fluctuated over the years. As with the situation with my ex-partner I had experienced anger and bargaining a number of times by trying to get back with him. Finally, I accepted that it was not meant to be, but I was also being held back because I was in denial for a number of years. The diabetes, however, I am still working on and am beginning to come to terms with it gradually.

I have found the courage and strength that was needed to confront my fears of speaking publicly and helping others to create confidence in themselves. I hid the fact for years that my ex had been unfaithful because I didn't want people to judge him or me. There was even a point when my daughter was blaming me for breaking up with her dad. I just accepted the blame rather than say anything as I felt she was too young and didn't want to taint the image she had of him. He eventually told her the truth and, although I was somewhat surprised, I was relieved that she knew. That was another secret that I no longer had to keep.

Hebrews 13 v 6 So we say with confidence, "The Lord is my helper; I will not be afraid. What can mere mortals do to me?" (NIV)

Strength and courage can be found in some of our most difficult moments. Jeremiah had no confidence in himself for he was just a youth, but God made him a prophet to the nations. Joshua also did not believe that he could take over the leadership from Moses, but God gave both Joshua and Jeremiah the ability and confidence to step out.

I believe that He will also give you the strength and courage to overcome situations if you are willing to take a step out in faith and believe in yourself for better things.

Success will never lower its standards to accommodate you. You have to raise your standards to achieve it. God provides food for every bird but not in its nest. Rise up to the challenges ahead of you and conquer your fears (Unknown)

Chapter 5

Christian Slaves

Exodus 1 v 14 So they ruthlessly made the people of Israel work as slaves and made their lives bitter with hard service, in mortar and brick and in all kinds of work in the field. In all their work they ruthlessly made them work as slaves. (ESV – English Standard Version)

Exodus 6 v 5–9 Moreover, I have heard the groaning of the people of Israel whom the Egyptians hold as slaves and I have remembered my covenant. Say therefore to the people of Israel, I am the Lord and I will bring you out from under the burdens of the Egyptians and I will deliver you from slavery to them and I will redeem you with an outstretched arm and with great acts of judgement. (ESV)

On my way home from work one evening I was reading the news about a play called *Slaves* that was being featured in London. The word 'slave' remained with me for some time raising the following question: Why are Christians still living as slaves, continuing to live in bondage even though Christ died for our freedom?

I believe we hold ourselves captive through our thoughts, behaviour and actions and I can honestly say that this has applied to me in my walk as a Christian. By holding onto unforgiveness we are slaves; by holding onto past hurts we are slaves; by holding onto past behaviours we are slaves. Depression, anxiety, anger, and low self-esteem have us bound up and we are still slaves, forgetting that we are Christians and are therefore free. We should be holding onto God for He is the healer, provider, restorer, comforter, Lord of Lords, the one and only Master whom we should serve at all times. He has made a covenant to us to deliver us from slavery and bring us into the land that He promised so that we are no longer bound or held captive by our former masters. If God has promised this to us and we have read it in his word, then the transition should be easy, shouldn't it? But it's obvious that as Christians we are struggling with this based on our behaviour. How do we really become free from our former ways? Slaves that have been bound and shackled so that we cannot escape our masters.

Slaves were branded to show who they belonged to. Their skin would be stamped with hot metal showing the emblem of their masters. Once they gained freedom, the marks were still there but they were given a new lease of life and opportunity to move forward. Even though they had been scarred this would not prevent them from progressing. Some slaves would move on whilst others would stay working for their former masters as they were fearful of the unknown. A lot of them were born into slavery and that way of life was the norm to them. Just as we have been born into sin, until you become a Christian you would not recognise that there is an alternative way to live. Although we were born into sin, Christ died for our transgressions, and by knowing and accepting Him as our Saviour we have been delivered from sin and have been set free. Therefore, the shackles have been removed and we are newly branded in Christ and have been sealed with His blood. We are new creations and the things of the past should be left behind us.

2 Corinthians 5 v 17 – Therefore if anyone is in Christ, he is a new creation. The old has passed away; behold the new has come. (ESV)

There are so many scriptures in the Bible telling us who we are and what God has done for us, yet we still struggle. As Christians, we are not of the world and should not be led by the flesh but by the Holy Spirit. However, everyday challenges can get in the way leading us to act in the flesh which affects our behaviour and thought process.

Romans 8 v 1–3 tells us *Therefore there is no condemnation (no adjudging guilty of wrong) for those who are in Christ Jesus, who live (and) walk not after the dictates of the flesh, but after the dictates of the Spirit. For the law of the Spirit of life (which is) in Christ Jesus (the law of our new being) has freed me from the law of sin and of death. For God has done what the Law could not do (its power) being weakened by the flesh (the entire nature of man without the*

Holy Spirit) sending his own son in the guise of sinful flesh and as an offering for sin, God condemned sin in the flesh (subdued, overcame deprived it of its power over all who accept that sacrifice. (AMP)

That's all I strive for but find it so hard to attain, and when I do, it is never consistent and is only for a season!

The Word also tells us that we have been transformed by the renewing of the mind (Medonoya). Why do we find it so hard to renew our minds? Why do we still feel caged in, going around in circles even though we have been freed from our former Master? Why are we still controlled by the masters of fear, anxiety, depression, anger, idolatry, bad habits, low self-esteem, and people? How do we find that peace and hold onto it both now and forever? Is it because we want to continue that way? Do we believe that is all we our worth and therefore deserve to be bound up? Maybe the following will give you an insight into why we cannot break free.

We are creatures of habit, but habits can be broken and there are millions of former drug addicts, alcoholics and many others who can testify to that. No doubt it was not easy for them to make that change and probably took lots of attempts before they finally broke free. When I was smoking weed I would often say I'm not going to have another spliff. However, I still found myself going back until one day I woke up disposing of everything that would tempt me. Even though I was still associating with people who did smoke, I was strong enough to abstain from it as I knew it served no real purpose in my life and was only holding me captive.

There is a story of an elephant that was shackled from a young age and could only go so far within the environment it was housed in. One day its master released the chains that bound it and yet the elephant that had now grown into an adult still remained within the confines not knowing that he was free to roam around. That was the only life the elephant knew. I assume that even as he got larger that he may have been able to break the chain and overpower his masters. Over the many years it is obvious that his mind had been programmed that he could not escape and I suppose he just gave up trying. Some of us don't even realise that we are free as we have been bound up for so long.

I know that I have been held captive to many situations, in particular staying in relationships or keeping friendships that were damaging to me. I had a vision and expectation of how my relationship with my daughter's father should have been. We were with one another until my daughter was five years old. He had been unfaithful to me during this time, however, I held on even though the relationship was strained. I did so many things to try and restore it back to what it formerly was, however, once trust is broken, it is difficult to get it back and eventually the relationship ended. It was very difficult for me to advance forward and, even though it was over, I still couldn't accept it. Who wants to raise a child on their own? That simply wasn't my plan. So, I waited in the hope that he would change his mind and want to create a family with me. I remained a slave to my emotions and wanted him to notice me but he never did see me as anything other than the mother of his child. I couldn't move forward with those chains binding me and eventually realised that I was the one holding myself captive. He had freed himself and I was trying to draw him back even though things probably wouldn't have changed even if we did get back together. It was as if I was purposefully punishing myself because I didn't expect anything better or different. All I had experienced through life was rejection and abuse, so why would there be anything better available to me? Finally, I accepted that it was not meant to be, recognising my worth and realising that I did not need him to complete me. I was determined to raise my daughter regardless of whether he was with me or not, and I was doing an amazing job. Eventually I re-adjusted my thought process and gained the strength to move forward, overthrowing the enemy's plan to keep me captive. Believe me, since I did that I have seen my life turn around completely and have a great sense of freedom. The chains have now been broken!

The Bible says that we are free and therefore we should not be condemning ourselves once we have given our lives over to Christ.

We have been freed from the law of sin and death. Maybe we seek gratification in the flesh, but when we live in the Holy Spirit then our outlook should be different. If we continue to live in the flesh then we will not be released from slavery and will not create the inner peace and freedom that we so desire.

Exodus 3 v 8–10 And the Lord said, I have surely seen the affliction of my people which are in Egypt, and have heard their cry by reason of their taskmasters; for I know their sorrows; And I am come down to deliver them out of the hand of the Egyptians, and to bring them up out of that land unto a good land and a large, unto a land flowing with milk and honey; unto the place of the Canaanites, and the Hittites, and the Amorites, and the Perizzites, and the Hivites, and the Jebusites. Now therefore, behold, the cry of the children of Israel is come unto me: and I have also seen the oppression wherewith the Egyptians oppress them. Come now therefore, and I will send thee unto Pharaoh, that thou mayest bring forth my people the children of Israel out of Egypt. (KJV)

As many struggles as the enslaved Israelites endured under Pharaoh, they were God's chosen people. They were not meant to be slaves but free, and although they were willing to accept their fate, God interceded on their behalf and brought them to their destiny. God will intercede on your behalf too and sees your suffering, but because we are His children He has already delivered us into a land flowing with milk and honey. God is the locksmith that will remove the chains. All we have to do is step out of them and walk into our destiny.

Are you ready to break those chains and release yourself from bondage?

Chapter 6

Race for Life

With confidence, you have won before you have started. Without confidence you are defeated before the race has begun.

If you have no confidence in self, you are twice defeated in the race of life. (Marcus Garvey, Jamaican political leader, publisher, journalist, entrepreneur)

In July 2014, I completed the 5k Race for Life (charity event) at Hyde Park with my daughter. This was my fourth time taking part. The first time I signed up with a friend in June 2008 and this was held at Hampstead Heath, a park I wasn't familiar with. We prepared separately for the race, training and building up stamina not knowing what obstacles were before us. But we were both determined to take part as we knew it was for a good cause. On the day of the race, my brother came along to support me and waited for me at the finish line. 5k is approximately three miles which is not very long but can feel so far when you don't know where you are going, what lies ahead and when you will see the finish line. It starts off easy but as you progress it becomes difficult (depending upon your stamina level). There were a number of hilly parts that we had to ascend and at one point I looked at my friend and said, "You know we're walking that right?" I knew my capabilities and decided not to watch others or care what they thought as we were all destined to reach the finish line. Although we had the same goal, everyone completed the course at their own pace. This was not a competition, but some people chose to race off ahead. When I finished, it was great to see my brother at the end, receive my medal and, of course, a bottle of water. I felt a great sense of achievement for completing it and was on a buzz for ages. Since then, I have completed the other three races at Hyde Park, which is a much easier course.

After the first time, I knew exactly what path it would follow and when the finish line would be drawing near. It is a much easier course to run, with no hills or obstacles on the pathway. The year I ran with my daughter, I was able to let her know what would be around the corner. Although there was a point, embarrassingly enough, when she went off ahead of me and beat me to the finish line. I won't tell you by how many minutes though, that is a secret I choose not to share.

What I am trying to say is we are all on a journey. Some journeys are easy as we know where we are going and already have things mapped out. We will probably have a plan in place and therefore have a starting point and know the obstacles that we will meet along the way to reach our final destination. It may be a route that we've already taken and can do it blindfolded without even thinking about it, travelling along in autopilot mode. For example, a journey into work that you do on a daily basis you may begin to become complacent and comfortable. But what do you do when the dynamics change and there are things you didn't anticipate such as road closures or your train line is down? What is your response to the unexpected event or obstacle that prevents you from getting to where you need to be? Do you panic or fly off the handle or do you stop and adopt a calm approach allowing yourself to think the options through? Will you need assistance along the way if you are not sure of the alternatives or which route to take?

The conditions and the storms we endure on our journey can create difficult situations and slippery slopes. Soldiers have to endure intense training through all types of conditions to prepare them for the battles that they will have to face. Professional athletes also have to endure this kind of training. Runners in particular have to train every day to build up stamina so that they can perform at their best for each competition they face. Each time they are hoping to get a better result. The race and the journeys that we face along the way may create obstacles that could make us fall or slow us down. God will give us a helping hand during the training and throughout the race, and it may come in the form of a friend or brethren who will encourage you. On our race for life (eternal life) sometimes we may get exhausted along the way, can't catch our breath and feel suffocated. Marathon runners hit a point in their twenty-six mile journey where they hit a brick wall and feel that they cannot go on. They are probably feeling burnt out and in pain, but they find a way to continue even though they may feel they want to throw in the towel and can't persevere. You probably wonder what the journey is all about especially when you feel that you aren't getting anywhere or gaining anything from it. It may be easier to opt for a route you already know. Should you continue at the pace you are going, you may find yourself burnt out. This may be your opportunity to sit out for a while to get a second breath, reenergise, refresh, and take a deep breath. Some of us may want to take a short cut to get there quicker, so we go off the designated course, which could lead to a dead end (T Junction). This will lead us to turn back to the point where we veered off course meaning that our race will take a little longer to complete.

As Christians, sometimes we want to get to this place a lot quicker so we try an alternative route, drifting away from God, believing that we know a better way to go as God's way is taking too long. We can't see where we are going and don't know when we will reach the end. Just as we might turn to a Sat Nav, map or ask someone to help us reach our destination. These things will provide us with all the information we need to continue our journey. Although at times you might turn to people who you think can help you but who are on a totally different journey to you and could lead you in the wrong direction. God has our paths already set out, so when we go astray and find ourselves lost, we will need to turn back to God who will put us back on track

Below are some examples of similarities in the Bible:

- Prodigal Son – He ran off ahead of his destiny thinking he knew better and that his chosen path would be the easy one. He became lost along the way and eventually he had no choice but to return to where he came from and start all over again.

- Jonah – Was given clear directions of where he needed to be but instead of going to Nineveh to deliver God's message, he took his own journey. Jonah believed that his way was the right way and so journeyed onto Tarshish trying to get away from the presence of the Lord. Because of his disobedience, he endured a storm on the ship. Sometimes this can happen when we draw further from God's presence. Eventually, he was thrown overboard being saved by the large fish and was in the belly of the fish for three days and three nights. That was his time to get back in the presence of God, rest, reflect and recharge for the journey that was before him. When the time was right he was ejected by the fish and set on the right path.

Throughout the race, you may have to travel through murky waters and endure intense heat (similar to the training ground for soldiers) but God says in *Isaiah 43 v 2 – When u pass through the waters, I will be with you and through the rivers, they shall not overwhelm you; when you walk through the fire you shall not be burned and the flame shall not consume you. (AMP)*

Imagine running the race with essential items such as water and probably an mp3 player to make the run more pleasurable and easier to bear. These items would be very easy to carry. But would you consider taking unnecessary items such as a rucksack filled with your laptop, mobile phone, books, photographs, change of clothing, your pets, make up (you get where I'm going with this). Basically, carrying extra baggage will weigh you down and make your journey a lot more difficult and will eventually become a burden. If we remove the excess baggage and just walk/run with the things that are important/necessary, then the race will be a lot easier. The excess baggage could be anxiety, money worries, loneliness, rejection, etc.

The following scriptures are trying to tell us to remove that baggage and offload them onto God.

Peter 5 v7 Cast all your anxiety on him because he cares for you (NIV)

Matt 11 v 28 Come unto me, all ye that labour and are heavy laden, and I will give you rest. (AMP)

What exactly are we hoping to receive at the end of the race? Salvation! Salvation means deliverance, redemption, rescue, recovery, escape, revitalisation, restoration, improvement. Amongst these things, we will also receive God's glory and a chance to be with Him and sit at His throne. Therefore, we should have a goal/purpose. However, a lot of people don't know what that is so we need to draw closer to God to gain an understanding of what that could be and also to learn something during the race.

What are the benefits of enduring and completing the race? Well, I received a medal at the end of each race which was my reward for taking part, and completing the race allowed me to raise money to help with cancer research.

The following scriptures highlight the rewards of being a Christian and why we should have endurance to run the race.

I Corinthians 9 v 24 – Do you not know that in a race all runners run, but only one receives the prize? So run that you may obtain it. Every athlete exercises self-control in all things. They do it to receive a perishable wreath, but we imperishable. So I do not run aimlessly; I do not box as one beating the air. But I discipline my body and keep it under control lest after preaching to others I myself should be disqualified. (ESV)

2 Timothy 4 v 7–8 – I have fought the good fight, I have finished the race, I have kept the faith. Now there is in store for me the crown of righteousness, which the Lord, the righteous Judge, will award to me on that day – and not only to me, but also to all who have longed for His appearing. (NIV)

Keep your eyes on the prize. The prize of Jesus Christ and eternal life. God is the redeemer and with Him there are great and substantial rewards, but we need to have constant faith and be willing to endure the race and all the pain that comes with it.

Hebrews 12 v 1 – Therefore since we are surrounded by so great a cloud of witnesses, let us also lay aside every weight and sin which clings so closely and let us run with endurance the race that is set before us. (ESV)

The road that we take as Christians is not an easy one and the paths may not be easy to travel along. Some may be extremely narrow, restricting our movement, making us feel under pressure – but if we remove some of the weight that is holding us back then we will be able to get through.

Romans 5 v 1-5–Therefore, since we have been justified by faith, we have peace with God through our Lord Jesus Christ. Through Him we have also obtained access by faith into this grace in which we stand we rejoice in hope of the glory of God. Not only that, but we rejoice in our sufferings, knowing that suffering produces endurance, and endurance produces character and character produces hope and hope does not put us to shame, because God's love has been poured into our hearts through the Holy Spirit who has been given to us. (ESV)

We are all going through our own personal struggles in this race for life and these scriptures can help us to persevere, give us the strength required to get through the storms, build our character and produce the hope within us that we will get through. Remember we are more than conquerors through Christ who strengthens us.

Part 2

Awakening

Chapter 7

Salvation

A s new Christians, we have the desire to live righteously, no longer giving into temptation but living solely to please the Lord. We should constantly be declaring our faith by letting people know we are saved, not being ashamed of Christ and trying to bring along others with us to experience the goodness of God and having eternal life through Him.

This can prove to be difficult with the trials and many temptations that we face, and as Christians I feel it is important to recognise that the trials will still come. The enemy will test our faith in God on many occasions. When we were living in sin, we didn't see any real issues with our lifestyles but when we are saved, the Holy Spirit will start to convict us and we will need to put aside the former things. Our behaviour/reactions to situations should be different, but oftentimes that isn't easy to do.

Salvation, means to deliver someone or something from impending danger. Salvation allows us to be delivered from sin and saves/rescues us from our current state, providing us with a new hope/outlook as to how we need to conduct our lives. Man is saved through the grace of God and not through our own doing/works as Ephesians 2 v 8–9 tells us. By seeking salvation and accepting Jesus as our personal Saviour we are released from sin and God starts to perform a work in us to direct and lead us away from temptation onto the path of righteousness. The Holy Spirit is then brought to life within us and convicts us of sin. We were delivered from sin through Christ dying for us.

Jesus was sent to Earth as a living sacrifice because we had been separated from God through Adam's disobedience when he ate of the Tree of Knowledge and died spiritually. When Jesus was sacrificed at Calvary we were then reconciled in fellowship with God through the Holy Spirit living within us so that we would then have a direct connection with Him. Each of us is a spirit with a soul and body and by being saved, the Holy Spirit becomes alive within us. Although the spirit has always been present, it is not until we accept Jesus Christ as our personal Saviour that the Holy Spirit becomes alive within us.

Upon being saved, new believers should seek to get baptised. This is an open declaration to others that we are Christians and it is an outward expression of the work that has taken place within us. It shows people that we have changed our former ways and we are dead to sin, and it symbolises the death and resurrection of Jesus Christ. It is an act of obedience to Christ and complies to the will of God. Jesus spoke to the disciples in Matthew 28:19–20 stating that they should go forth to nations baptising them in the name of the Father, Son and Holy Spirit and that we should observe the things that He commanded. Baptism is also openly declaring our love for Jesus and a promise that we will be disciples for the Lord and is therefore not optional but a command of Jesus. Through our love for Jesus, we should be ready to obey Him.

I understood the steps I needed to take once I received Salvation, however, it took me almost nine years after being saved to take the step of being baptised. Making a commitment is not one I take lightly and I don't like to play church. It is like becoming a parent where we are committed to taking on the needs of our children and is a role that should not be taken for granted. It is a big change in our lives, which requires hard work, perseverance, endurance, reasoning, and not forgetting countless sleepless nights. Your life just isn't the same and at times you may want to quit, but you have a responsibility. Being a Christian is almost like having a binding contract between you and your child which you cannot renege from. Baptism is about making a commitment to God by putting away the old life and taking on a new one.

When I got baptised it was a water baptism which required a full immersion rather than a sprinkling of water that takes place within some churches. The full immersion symbolises the death of Christ by going under the water and when we arise out of the water will represent the newness of life and the resurrection of Christ. This was a new day for me where members of my family and friends were there to witness my declaration to God.

Being a Christian does not end there and prayer plays a pivotal part. Although we are saved, we need to build a greater relationship with God by communicating with Him and prayer helps us to achieve this. Prayer is not just about making requests for our needs to be met and should not be done as a selfish act. We should be thanking God for the things He has already done in our lives. Praising Him for who He is and recognising that without Him we would not be here. Being a child of God means that we are walking in faith and that God is working on our behalf. Prayer can have an impact on what will happen in our lives. Although God has already purposed our lives and the direction it will take, He wants us to rely upon Him. We should seek Him with all of our heart and He will answer our requests but only within His time.

Praying to God is not as difficult as people believe. We can communicate with Him through our thoughts, hearts and by talking to Him as we would to a friend or family member. It doesn't always need to be a drawn-out process; simple prayers can be just as effective. Prayer can be used when we are feeling at our wits' end. God may step in to answer these quickly and other times we may need to wait as He is trying to teach us something. During this time of waiting, we are also being taught lessons on humility, patience and wisdom as well as testing our faith in Him. Not all of our prayers will be answered if it is not God's will for us. If we have unconfessed sin in our lives this can create a barrier between us and God and some prayers will not be answered. We must not only look to prayer when we are experiencing difficulties but also when things are going well for us. It is essential that we pray at all times without ceasing and confess our sins to the Lord seeking His forgiveness and deliverance. As mentioned previously, prayer should not be used for selfish reasons and we should also pray for others if they have a need. God wants us to build a relationship with Him. As well as us praying to God and speaking to Him, we also need to be quiet to hear His voice. He can come to you in a gentle whisper, through dreams or using others to deliver a message on His behalf. This is all a part of Him making you aware of His presence; letting you know your prayer has been heard.

We should seek salvation to give us a new life and change of attitude. Once we have been saved, the spirit of God will become alive in us and we will only want to live to please Him. We are made in God's image and are representing Him to the world. Therefore we need to live righteously in accordance to His will and purpose.

Baptism is an open declaration to the world that we are committed to Him, have been taken into a new life and have shed our former ways.

Prayer is communicating and appreciating God for who He is and for what He has done and can do in our lives. All of these things come together to give us faith and hope and to help us experience a new outlook on life through Christ.

Taking these steps opened up a new level of understanding in regards to my journey with the Lord. By putting God first, my life had been enhanced along with my relationship with Him and my spiritual growth. It has been vitally important to put my trust in Him as only God can deliver me to a life of righteousness. Don't get me wrong though, I am not saying that I haven't experienced temptations and trials since being saved or baptised. I have given you little snippets of some of the things I have experienced. However, when I do make mistakes I acknowledge them and ask God for His forgiveness. That does not mean that we should fall into the trap of continually making mistakes. Knowingly committing them and believing it's ok because God will forgive us is not a smart path to follow. We know that God is a forgiving God and because He knows our hearts we shouldn't consider

Him to be taken for a fool. With the mistakes that I have made, I have felt convicted and therefore try my hardest to make my wrongs right with Him. It is a struggle at times and I have still found myself giving into temptation.

As I have mentioned before, the walk as a Christian is not an easy one to undertake and should not be viewed as such. It will take a lot of commitment and sacrifice.

Are you prepared to take that step?

Chapter 8

A New Perspective

Luke 10 v 38–42 – Now it came to pass, as they went, that he entered into a certain village; and a certain woman named Martha received him into her house. And she had a sister called Mary, which also sat at Jesus' feet and heard his word. But Martha was cumbered about much serving and came to him and said Lord, dost thou not care that my sister hath left me to serve alone? Bid her therefore that she help me. And Jesus answered and said unto her, Martha, Martha, thou art careful and troubled about many things. But one thing is needful, and Mary hath chosen that good part, which shall not be taken away from her. (KJV)

As part of the Women's Ministry Service at my local church, the leader of the team asked a few of the female members, myself included, to do a talk to the congregation on what the above scripture meant to us. During my time of preparation, I reflected on the scripture and the words "new perspective" were dropped into my spirit. I feel inclined to share my thoughts on this particular scripture in the hope that you may start to see things from a new perspective. I hope that it will change your approach to situations and distinguish the things that are important in life.

When I started to deliver my message, I firstly moved some members of the congregation out of their seats. These were members that normally take the same seat every Sunday in church; creatures of habit. Once they were settled I then went on to explain what this scripture meant to me.

I commenced by saying that we all have a bit of Martha and Mary within us. Almost like a Jekyll and Hyde personality, but oftentimes we tend to lean towards Martha. Meaning that we busy ourselves with things that are not always necessary or important at the time such as keeping home, tidying, washing. We simply can't keep still. We feel that something always needs our attention. This can become the norm for us and because of the way we have programmed ourselves, this outlook may prevent us from giving time to more important things such as family, relationships with others or health. The neglect of these things can be to our detriment.

In the summer of 2015, I was hospitalised for a week. On the first weekend of July, I decided to go to a local restaurant and sat outside in the sunshine whilst having a bite to eat and drinking sangria with the family. When I got home in the evening, I started experiencing pain in my inner thigh and on the Sunday morning I arose and felt very feverish. I put it down to suffering heat stroke and carried on with my normal household duties. That night I was in significant pain and my leg had started to swell but I refused to go to A&E as I expected the wait to be a long one. Instead I made a decision to go the following day after work. Monday morning I arose and went to work, even though I was in pain and experiencing cold sweats. I finally called the doctor's office to make an appointment for that evening and upon seeing them I was sent immediately to A&E. Before I knew it, I was being admitted to the hospital where I had been informed that I had something called cellulitis which had affected my bloodstream. Being a diabetic they couldn't run the risk of letting me go home and as you might imagine I was in shock. There I was one day ok and by the end of that week I was undergoing minor surgery to remove the infection from my thigh.

Things just happened so quickly and I simply wasn't prepared for it, I was in a complete panic when I was told I was to be admitted. My daughter was home alone and I still had things to do and was also worried about having to call in sick again. Fortunately, mum was on hand to take over. My daughter was amazing during that period; she was staying at mum's, going to school, returning home each evening to feed the pets and also visiting me at the hospital. I remember coming around after surgery and just giving thanks to God that I made it through. To be perfectly honest I was so scared, especially when I was being asked questions about the diabetes and my blood pressure and signing a waiver form before undergoing the operation. Although it was minor surgery, I started to panic thinking I could die and not be there for my daughter, so was truly thankful that I had woken up. I was in hospital for a week and upon my release was told to rest to allow time for healing. The surgery was on my inner thigh, which made it very difficult for me to get around, but this did not hinder me when I got home. I found it so hard to completely rely on others to help me so I could get the rest I needed. I still felt that I had a duty to continue performing my role, keep home, be a mother and ensure there was a cooked meal for my daughter when she returned home from school. Even during this time, some of the people I believed would be there to help me ended up letting me down. Admittedly I was a little disappointed. So rather than ask them for help, I resentfully got on with what I needed to do. But by not submitting myself to others, asking for help and being vulnerable, this delayed the healing process and I was signed off work for six weeks in total. The wound became re-infected and I was given additional antibiotics to treat this. I am not saying that we should keep a dirty home or neglect our duties and responsibility, but we need to identify what is important and what can wait.

Martha may have been busying herself because she was running away from something. Perhaps she needed validation from Jesus, needed to be seen in His eyes as valuable; maybe she always lived in Mary's shadow and was trying to 'prove' herself. Maybe she was trying to show Mary up. We don't know what her secret needs were just like we don't know the innermost needs of the people around us. But each of us has something inside us that we are struggling to balance or validate. I am aware of people doing just that, myself included. Sometimes, when we are built that way, we can see people relaxing and enjoying themselves whilst we are running around like a headless chicken. Because we *believe* there are many things that need to be done this can lead to frustration and resentment. Which was the case with

Martha (Luke 10 v 40). Martha was busy serving and wanted some assistance as she was feeling cumbered. She felt frustrated, angered and probably vexed that Mary was sitting down enjoying herself, relaxing and chilling out with Jesus. Maybe there was a bit of envy, as whilst doing all of these things she was not experiencing the joy and peace that Mary was receiving sitting with God. Martha's soul was troubled whilst Mary was receiving nourishment for hers.

Verse 40 of this scripture says that Martha was cumbered. To be cumbered means to be weighed down with many duties or distracted by many things and we have probably all experienced days like that.

There was a period of time when I felt really exhausted. Any parent will know what it is like juggling many things such as school clubs, homework, and collection from child minders as well as working full time. I even had compressed hours at one point where I would work 35 hours in four days having Fridays off so I could drop off and collect my daughter from school and catch up with housework. My days would be very long and on those four days I felt rushed. I remember coming home one evening and my Daughter said to me, "Mummy I spend more time at school and with Aunty Susan than I do with you". As a single parent, there is also an extra added pressure to make sure that you are available for your child's every need. My weekends were barely ever free and when I did get an opportunity to go out with friends or family to relax I was always too exhausted. I remember returning from work one evening and I felt totally burnt out having no energy, drive or motivation. I walked to the end of the platform to await my train and slid down the wall, put myself in a crouching position and cupped my head in my hands. A lady approached me and asked me if I was okay and the poor thing probably thought I was contemplating jumping onto the track. I looked up at her from my position and said, "You know one of those days when you have just had enough? Well, this is that day!" I had simply had enough of the multiple duties I had to undertake, felt unsupported and was feeling cumbered.

Martha in this situation felt the need to express these feelings to Jesus. When she complained to Him about her responsibility and Mary's lack of support, I believe she expected Jesus to agree with her, which is what most of us do, waiting for people to pity us and support what we say to justify our argument. But most of the time these situations are created by ourselves simply because we are juggling too many things and trying to be the martyr. Martha did not feel comfortable doing anything else but serving and believed that Mary should do the same. In verses 41–42 of this scripture Jesus' response was *"Martha, Martha thou art careful and troubled about many things; But one thing is needful; and Mary hath chosen that good part, which shall not be taken away from her.* Jesus didn't support her thoughts but instead told her to view things from a different perspective, stop busying herself and basically quit complaining about what *she had chosen* to take on.

Martha was overwhelmed with all her duties and responsibilities, but *Matthew 11 v 28 says Come to me all ye that labour and are heavy laden and I will give you rest (KJV).* After my train station experience, I had to re-evaluate all the things that I was doing that were burning me out, view things differently, prioritise things in my life and learn to delegate some duties to others to allow myself more rest.

God isn't going to come in and clean up your house and there are certain things that we cannot avoid doing. However, God can cleanse our souls, give us a new vision and help us to see things from another perspective. All we have to do is take time out from our busy schedules and spend time with Him and He will provide us with the support that we need.

In closing my message at the service, I posed the following questions to the congregation and you may benefit from reflecting on them also.

1. Are you ready to view things from a different perspective?
2. Are you Martha or Mary?
3. Where would you rather be, heavy-laden or resting in Jesus?

Admittedly, on the few occasions when I was feeling extremely exhausted and was asking God for rest, maybe this was His way of telling me to be more like Mary, where I ended up being hospitalised, signed off work but had time to rest in Him. However, neither of these women did anything wrong as both were serving God and making sacrifices to Him.

Some of us choose to stay in the same situation, but familiarisation can breed contempt which was similar to the way Martha must have felt. Unfortunately, at the end of my talk the members went back to their original seats, but I do hope that they received the message I was trying to convey and are looking at things from a new perspective.

Chapter 9

Relationships

We do not travel through life on our own. Although at times we may feel lonely we are not by ourselves. We have to interact with people along the way, some just for a short period of time and others for a life time. Relationships are built with many people along the way, such as family, friends, work colleagues, mentors and teachers. Some of these people will get an understanding of who you are over the years. They will think they 'know' you and will form an opinion based on what they've experienced with you. Who they *think* you are is based equally on their own perspective and personal history. But no one can ever really know the true heart of another except God. Why is this? Because as people, we are judgemental. Our judgements are based on what we know, see, hear, and intuitively feel. And since we often do not let out our true heart, others cannot know it, therefore their judgements may be somewhat inaccurate.

I was very quiet as a child and this was owing to the fact that I was bullied and didn't believe that I had a voice. I was trying to protect others but was unable to protect myself by speaking up. I did have fun and liked to entertain people but that was just a way of making people believe I was ok.

We moved home when I was about seven years old and that's when dad moved in with us. He stayed for seven years, and at the age of 14, things changed in my life. To be honest, my siblings and I were happy that he was going due to all the pain and upset he had caused us and mum during that time. His leaving, however, did have an impact on us, which we each dealt with in different ways. Dad had three other children outside of the marriage. I have an older half-sister in Grenada who was dad's first child before he met my mum and moved to England.

I also have a younger half-sister and half-brother. Dad had an outside family and would leave us certain evenings of the week to look after my younger half-sister whilst her mother went to work. He probably stayed with us for three days out of the week. It was a horrible situation to be in and I remember having parents' evening in my 2nd year at Secondary school. On this occasion, mum had to work so dad was the only parent available to attend. We went to the school and all he wanted to see was the English and Maths teachers. Never once did he express an interest in what subjects I liked, which at the time was Art and I was doing particularly well in it. At one point, he seemed a bit irritated as the English teacher was busy, so he went to see my History teacher until the English teacher became available. To be honest with you, I don't think he actually paid any attention to what they were saying. When we finally got a chance to see the English teacher, fortunately she had good things to say about my progress, otherwise that would have been another story in itself. We left the school promptly where he took me to the bus stop and didn't even wait for me to get the bus. It seems that he was so desperate not to be late to look after my half-sister and he didn't even call to see whether I got home. I held that in my mind for so many years afterwards. Eventually I told him when I got older that I didn't feel I was important to him, but dad being dad casually swept it under the carpet. This is something that he would normally do when confronted with situations he did not want to deal with. Often his response to situations like this would be "Well I gave your mother money to look after you all". And at some point during our relationship I told him that you can't always throw money at things. Money or material things for that matter cannot replace a relationship and that is all I wanted from my dad.

When dad left, we all grieved in our own ways and unfortunately I started to experiment with cannabis and alcohol. Looking back on that period of my life, I now have an understanding of what pushed me in that direction, although at the time I just thought I was having a bit of fun. But what had led me to that place was the loss of my father and the breakdown of a family. I had also been rejected by friends at school and didn't feel like I fitted in anywhere. I eventually found a group of people that I used to hang out with at lunch times and after school where we would just smoke and drink Canei or Thunderbird. My behaviour led me to play truant at school, lose focus on my studies and go down the wrong path. I would take my pocket money and go halves with a friend to purchase a £5 bag of weed between us and get high. I believed at the time it made me somehow cool and tough and I would be accepted. It allowed me to escape and create an image that was so far from the truth of who I really was. But looking back, I was weak and this was a way of me forgetting about my worries. Not once did I really think God could have been my strength and the answer to my problems throughout that time. Where would He fit in? And the few friends I did have would probably start to shun me. My siblings and parents didn't have a clue what I was doing. However, I know that God had His hands on me. The paths that I have seen other people go down and their outcomes have been completely different to mine. Some are fully dependent on drugs and alcohol, experienced physical abuse in relationships, have major mental health issues, and sadly some have died. Fortunately, I was one of the lucky ones and I am truly thankful knowing that He has my life in His hands and delivered me from my ignorance. What I was trying to do was to ignore my feelings/emotions by doing these things.

I was also very angry for a long time. The people that knew me would often call me ignorant because of my behaviour at times. I would flip out at the smallest thing, cursing, at times being very irrational and somewhat aggressive. I know I was acting out what people were continually saying about me. When I was called ignorant it would only incite more ignorance in me and this would then be unleashed. It was a vicious cycle that I needed to be released from. After a while, I had to look at myself and take a closer look at my behaviour. If so many people were saying the same things about me, especially those who knew me, there had to be some element of truth in it. I realised that the hurt and rejection I had experienced during my youth had a severe impact on me so I created a wall. This was my wall of protection: to attack before I was attacked. There were so many issues that I hadn't dealt with and so many emotions I didn't want to face, which was one of the reasons, I suppose, that led me to smoking, and strangely enough one of the reasons why I gave it up. Although it seemed fun in the beginning, as time went on I began to become paranoid. Sometimes it made me think about things in the past, that I honestly wanted to forget. I was scared of confronting these things, so one day I literally and figuratively woke up and said this is it, I'm giving up smoking weed. And that was the end of that.

When I got saved, my outlook changed as well as my personality. I became a little bit lighter, choosing not to over react to situations. There was definitely an adjustment in my approach to things and people. There are times when people still try to label me in the same way, but I know I have changed considerably because of the way I now deal with issues. There are times I may slip and it may just be 1 time out of 100, but I recognise that people will try to keep you in a box not wanting you to move out of it. They cannot accept that you have changed and always expect the same behaviour from you. So, the one time that you do slip up they want you to believe that you haven't or cannot change and normally start their sentences with 'you always' rather than 'you used to'. At times I may put them in their place, but other times I ignore it and don't let it dwell in my psyche for too long as I know that I have made significant progress. Do not fall into that trap either, this is simply an attack of the enemy who wants you to believe that you haven't changed and that you are not making any progress.

Through these experiences, I have managed to control my anger and keep it under subjection, but occasionally it raises its ugly head. I now have the wisdom to dig deeper so I can understand where it is coming from and try to deal with it a lot quicker rather than let it fester creating toxicity in my life. I am learning to preserve that energy for the battles that are really important and believe me when I say I am still facing them.

I have restored my relationship with my father. I no longer blame him for my past but embrace him in my future. At one point of time, I said that when he passed away I would not miss him at all as he had been absent for a long period of my life. My dad is now in his 70's and one day he called to say he was unwell and was in hospital. Immediately after I put down the phone, I cried so hard not wanting anything to happen to him. I prayed to God that He would make him okay and give him a clean bill of health. I realised at that moment that I truly loved my father and would miss him. Even if we didn't spend much time together throughout my life, he was still a part of it. I have now accepted him for who he is and no longer pass blame. He is my father and I love him unconditionally. Apportioning blame for the rest of his or my life would not make a difference, but forgiving and removing my anger would.

Just as God the Father loves me with my imperfections, I should also love my father with his. Our relationship may not be perfect, but it is as it should be and I no longer hold anger or resentment towards him. I even wrote him a letter, expressing my feelings towards him. These were not negative feelings that related to what he didn't do, but letting him know that I was grateful for the things that he did do. I wanted him to know that I was looking forward to the remaining time we have together and building upon our relationship. Even if it is a two minute conversation on the phone every few weeks and seeing him once every few months, I appreciate every moment we have together.

I have learnt to value myself and realise that everyone has at least one insecurity within themselves. Even if it is with their appearance or the fear of being rejected. I recognise that nobody is perfect but some people are just better than others at covering up their insecurities. Hidden behind that confident image is somebody who is suffering silently.

I definitely created a picture to people that I was coping, when deep down inside I was broken. I was continually blaming myself believing that I was not good enough. I would constantly seek others' approval, staying in toxic relationships/friendships that weren't healthy just because I didn't value myself. Accepting people's abuse, settling for sexual relationships that weren't meaningful and tolerating friends/family that took advantage of my kind nature. I now realise that this was not helping me in any way and was only affecting my self-esteem, exacerbating my tendency to undervalue myself.

It's time to ask yourself the following questions:

- What is it that needs repairing within you?
- Are there any broken relationships that need repairing?
- Are you willing to accept people for who they are and that no matter what you try to do they might not change?
- Are you willing to be the one to take the step and create that change?
- Are you willing to forgive yourself and others knowing we are all struggling with something?

By taking the step to look deeper into yourself, you will be making a change in the right direction. You will find that inner peace and freedom you have been yearning for. I did just that and I am so glad that I am not in the place that I used to be.

You may not have had the perfect start in life, but there is nothing to say that the middle and the end cannot be better. If you are not happy with the chapter you are in right now, grab a hold of the pen and start to re-write the script. Remember to change your perspective of the past, forgive yourself and others, transform yourself by viewing with new eyes, and know that, as you deal with others, we are all coming from a different perspective.

Chapter 10

Rejection

Dealing with rejection is not an easy thing and over the years I have experienced a lot of it. Experiencing rejection by my father, friends, ex-boyfriends, and family made me believe that I was not good enough or worthy enough to be loved. However, I have discovered over time that this is not actually the case.

My daughter had been experiencing issues at school where her peers were excluding her from things and saying nasty things about her and it honestly grieved me as a parent to watch her endure similar things that I had as a child. She couldn't understand why they were picking her out and she then began to feel ostracised. People can be so cruel and don't actually realise the affect that their behaviour and actions are having on the other person. I have always taught her to think about others feelings and her behaviour towards them, yet she was experiencing these things, and just like me she is the kind of person who likes to fight for the underdog. As well as advising the school what was going on, the only other thing I could do as a parent to help my child was to reassure her that she is loved by her family, is beautiful, bright, amazing, and a strong individual. I also told her that these children didn't really know who they were and were probably suffering from low self-esteem themselves and the only way they could build themselves up was by putting others down. I prayed for her every morning and hoped that when she returned home in the evening that her day was a good one.

Having watched her experience this kind of rejection from Primary to Secondary school, I knew how it felt and didn't want her to suffer in the same way I had. It was painful to watch, especially when I had to constantly console her and wipe her tears on numerous occasions, literally forcing her to go to school and reassuring her that it would get better. I could see it was having an impact on her wellbeing and asked God why my daughter had to suffer. All I could hear was, "Why not?", and as you could imagine I was not too happy with that response. I angrily responded saying, "Because she is my daughter, she is only a child and you are meant to be protecting her. It's too much for her to bear and enough is enough." I was annoyed with God for allowing her to go through this. But through my prayers I know that He recognised that I was struggling and all I can remember was one day hearing the words, "Just look after yourself and I will take care of her". Those words gave me great comfort and I left it in His hands and took my focus away from the situation.

All parents want to protect their children and if she is meant to be God's child then why wasn't He doing His job? I remember getting the confirmation of being pregnant, I was so excited and protected her whilst she was in my stomach. Eventually I brought her home, caring for her, making sure all dangerous objects were removed out of her way, taking her to nursery for the first time where she was so eager. I watched her walk through the school gates and then couldn't do anything more to protect her during the times she wasn't with me or prevent her from being hurt by others. I realised that I could only take her as far as the school gates and couldn't sit with her throughout her school day, and though my spirit was with her and I prayed for her throughout, this was something that she had to discern and understand for herself. As much as I tried to affirm her, she needed to affirm herself which is really what God does with us, He can only bring us so far but we have to come to the realisation by ourselves as to who we are, even though He has been guiding and affirming us all along.

My daughter is a tough cookie but there is only so much a person can take without thinking that they are the problem. I just didn't want her to go through the same things as I did, knowing how it affected my childhood and self-esteem. I felt her pain and just wanted to take it away. She kept returning to these people as she felt there was nowhere else to go. I hope that gradually she will realise that she doesn't need to compromise who she is just to be accepted.

These situations can be really damaging to a person's ego and outlook on life. Oftentimes, the people who are inflicting this behaviour on others don't actually realise the consequences of their actions. This may lead some people to self-harm, turn to alcohol, become abusive, turn into bullies, and worse still, have suicidal thoughts. Unfortunately, some people have followed these suicidal thoughts through, leaving a void in the lives of those who loved them. It is something that we all have to endure throughout our lives and all we really want is to be loved and accepted. This doesn't always have to be an experience like the ones my daughter and I suffered. It could include being rejected for countless jobs that you felt you were qualified for, which could in turn make you feel devalued, demotivated and have a major impact on your self-worth.

After the situation arose with my daughter, I then started to think about Jesus' journey and how he was rejected by many. Even today this is still happening. However, that didn't prevent Him from living out His purpose. He rose up against these characters because He knew what he was sent on Earth to do and did not allow the negative things people said deter Him. He continued even when there were doubters. Eventually I understood what God meant when he asked, "Why not?" regarding my daughter. Jesus had been cursed and rejected by people, but never lost His focus, continuing in the face of adversity. Although He was rejected and humiliated by people He continued His onward journey for He was the son of God and His life was not dictated or governed by man. But He also found it in Himself to forgive His offenders along the way. I never rejected my daughter from birth and never expected anyone to do the same, but God knowingly sent His son Jesus to Earth aware of the rejection that He would face for us. Although we may face rejection from others, we need to know who we are and what our purpose is whilst on this Earth, but as a child it may be hard for us to comprehend.

Having experienced rejection in my life where I felt rejected by my father, friends and partners, sometimes I would still continue to pursue my ex-partner's in the hope that my perseverance would win them over and I would be accepted by them even though I knew that they were not right for me. I even went through a very long grieving process with my daughter's father because I couldn't accept that he didn't want to be with me. I just couldn't understand why I was subjecting myself to so much pain, pursuing him even though he clearly didn't want to be with me. It was crazy of me to think that someone could respect me if I was acting so needy. Jesus did not beg anyone to accept Him and nor should we.

Jesus understood the reasons why He was being rejected. He knew that those who were persecuting Him had no understanding of who He was. Nor did they understand their own motivations for behaving the way they did. They simply went by the conventional wisdom of the time and their own insecurities and fears. In the same way, we must try to understand the motivation behind why others treat us the way they do, whether it's good or not so good. Some people who come from a background of hurt will try to hurt others. If they are insecure, they will try to build themselves up by putting others down. They will steal your energy to make themselves bigger. That doesn't mean you must continue to keep them in your lives. It means that you must realize that the problem is often within the spirit of the persecutor, not the persecuted. Knowing this, you can therefore step back and see the situation from a new perspective.

When my parents got divorced it was a strange period for us all. When we found out, one of the first things we said to mum was to just take half of dad's money as we felt she deserved it. We only looked at things from a superficial perspective. Never once did I think about how mum really felt. Dad never came around to discuss it with us. I suppose in his mind he felt it had nothing to do with us. That this was a divorce between two individuals and therefore should not have any impact on us. However, years later, he decided to get remarried to the woman who had been the thorn in my family's side for all of those years. For this occasion he felt inclined to visit and tell us about this looming wedding and also had the audacity to extend an invitation to us. I remember the day so vividly. My sister and I were in the kitchen when he arrived and proceeded to share his good news. My sister got up and upon walking out of the room bluntly told him she wouldn't be going. I was washing the dishes and responded very sarcastically. I told him that he didn't tell us he was getting divorced, so why did he feel the need to tell us he was getting married. I have a bit of a twisted side to me where I will make people feel uncomfortable in situations by challenging them. With my dad being the kind of person who just looks at the surface and brushes things under the carpet, I wanted to see him squirm. I wanted him to feel what we were feeling and confront the issues at hand. This is a technique I use a lot on people and that may be an area that I also need to work on through my Christian journey. However, it did have an impact and dad was insistent that he really wanted us to attend. He looked extremely disappointed. I said he should be happy regardless of whether we were there or not, but I would most definitely not be in attendance. He left there looking forlorn and to be honest, at the time, I was glad. On the day when he finally got married, my sister was travelling to Barbados with my niece and mum and I took them to the airport. I remember mum saying in the car, "Your Dad will be getting married soon" and I just kissed my teeth, trying to ignore her comment. However, when we both got home we went to our bedrooms and I remember crying so hard for the remainder of the day. I felt so sad and rejected. Even though he had left the family home many years before, this was my dad, whom had dropped us and decided to create another family. I don't think mum and I saw one another until the next day. My friend called later that evening and I told her that dad had got married that day and expressed how I was feeling so cut up. However, I also recognised that if I felt that way then mum must have been completely broken by it. I can only imagine that she was in her room crying just like I was and probably feeling rejected also. In the room next door to mine was an amazing woman that had sacrificed so many years with a man, raising his children, taking his name, enduring so much pain only to be replaced by someone else. Although I have never been married, I knew what it was like to make a sacrifice for someone, having your heart broken and experiencing that feeling of abandonment.

It is important to remember, however, that although you experience rejection it should not be taken personally. Being able to bear this can build up your resilience and help you to become stronger. Don't get me wrong, it doesn't mean that it won't affect you but it shouldn't prevent you from living your life. Do not forget those people in your life that have been your supporters and have shown you unconditional love. Recognise the good things about yourself, learn to love yourself, flaws and all.

I also make reference to the verse below in **Chapter 4 'Feelings'.**

1 Peter 5 v 8–10 Be alert and of sober mind. Your enemy the devil prowls around like a roaring lion looking for someone to devour. Resist him, standing firm in faith, because you know that the family of believers throughout the world is undergoing the same kind of suffering. And the God of all grace who called you to his eternal glory in Christ, after you have suffered a little while, will himself restore you and make you strong, firm and steadfast. (NIV)

If you allow the enemy who rejected you to have control over your thoughts, you will continue to be vulnerable. Eventually you will become so consumed and overwhelmed by your emotions leading to all sorts of issues in your life. This scripture is saying to stand firm in your faith and not to give up hope as others have experienced the same. Which was the case with my daughter and I, and by going through similar situations when I was younger I was able to help and guide her through.

Growing up, I didn't realise I had a voice and should have been able to say *no* to things that I didn't feel comfortable with. That I could go against the grain, that I was worthy of something better and didn't have

Broken, Not Beyond Repair | Karen Holder

to accept what people said about me or believe that their opinions had any validity. I compromised who I was on many occasions to please people just so I could fit in with the hope they would like me. Even when I behaved that way it made no difference. So, I have now decided to be me and people can either take it or leave it. Their opinions do not matter as I know who I am as a person, what God thinks of me and what I mean to Him. I am a royal diadem in His hands and a precious jewel in His sight.

Isaiah 62 v 3 You will be a crown of splendour in the Lord's hand, a royal diadem in the hand of your God. (NIV)

I shall never be rejected by God as He is my Heavenly Father who watches over me and only has my best interests at heart. I can say that things started to improve for my daughter and she is so much happier and has more confidence. All I had to do was as God directed, which was to look after myself and He would take care of her. I put my complete faith in God believing that He would do as promised for He is faithful to His word. The following scripture reminds us of this;

Numbers 23 v 19 God is not a man, that He should lie, Nor a son of man, that He should repent. Has He said, and will He not do it? Or has He spoken and will He not make it good and fulfill it? (AMP)

Once you place your trust in Him and stand upon His word, things can change. Remember that you can overcome any obstacle if you pray and continue to have hope. Now if that is not a revelation or testimony then I don't know what is.

Chapter 11

Forgiveness

atthew 18 v 21–22 Then Peter came to Him and asked, "Lord, how many times will my brother sin against me and I forgive him and let it go? Up to seven times?" 22 Jesus answered him, "I say to you, not up to seven times, but seventy times seven. (AMP)

"To tolerate someone else's mistake is one thing. To forgive them is even greater." (Unknown)

Forgiveness is a very challenging thing for many people and like me you have probably found yourself having to forgive people on many occasions. Sometimes it is easier to do than others. As a Christian, I recognise that unforgiveness is a sin. As well as it being a sin it can cause more damage to you than the person who may have offended you. These people probably aren't aware that they have done anything wrong and are walking around oblivious to the fact that you are carrying these feelings. We all make mistakes and we are not all sinless.

I had one person who was causing me so much upset. We had very heated conversations, exchanged a lot of words and some of them were not so nice. They just couldn't understand my point of view, we were fighting ignorance with ignorance and so the battle continued for some time. I felt that their actions and the words used towards me were deeply offensive and I honestly wanted to seek revenge. I couldn't stand being around them, hear their name and where possible would find ways to avoid them. Every time they were in my presence a burning rage would stir inside of me taking away my joy and peace. Being a Christian, I knew that this was not the right way to live. They had done many things to me over a period of time and I always found myself trying to resolve the issues and make amends. Which was pretty much the story of my life. I always felt I had to apologise to people even if I wasn't in the wrong, but this was just too much.

I recall being in the house one evening and starting a conversation with God. I said to Him that I couldn't find it in my heart to forgive the person, so if this is something that He wanted me to do then He would have to fix it. Then I left it there with Him to resolve. Amazingly, He turned it around where I forgave the person, humbling myself and was able to talk to them about how I felt. Because of my approach, they began to understand my point of view and I, in turn, was open to hear what they had to say. This allowed us both to move forward from there. It wasn't easy but through God's help I was able to do this and resume a peaceful relationship. In that time, He opened my ears, eyes and my heart, giving me wisdom and understanding and teaching me the art of humility.

Matthew 18 v 21–22 specifically numbers the amount of times we should forgive a person. Seven times is a lot, but seventy times seven is too many times if you ask me. How many times would you allow someone to take advantage of your good nature, before you say enough is enough and you cancel them out of your life? Now we have been told what to do and what is right, but still find it difficult. However, God will continually forgive us of our sins.

I have identified four key areas where forgiveness may need to take place in our lives as well as giving a few scenarios where the unforgiveness may have arisen.

Four possible areas of releasing yourself and seeking forgiveness are listed below; these can be carried out in any particular order.

1. Forgiving others – the person/people you have had the issue with
2. Forgiving yourself – for holding unforgiveness in your heart towards someone who offended you, or maybe in this particular situation you could have been the offender, so you feel guilty and need to ask for forgiveness

3. Forgiving God – How many times have you been angry and upset with God for allowing you to experience situations and you feel like you can't forgive Him for this?

4. Forgiveness from God – Seeking forgiveness for all of your sins (this should be done on a continual basis)

Below are a few examples of where we could be carrying unforgiveness in our hearts and the stages that may need to be followed to release us.

Scenarios:

Abused

- Forgiving others – the abuser for taking advantage of you
- Forgiving yourself – you may blame yourself and feel that you were at fault and deserved to be treated in such a way
- Forgiving God – for allowing you to experience this as you believed He was meant to protect you

Bereavement

- Forgiving others – someone who may not have been supportive, may have said the wrong thing during this time – Or forgiving the person who has passed on. Maybe the death was brought on by them not living the perfect lifestyle
- Forgiving yourself – maybe you weren't there enough for them and felt you could have done more to prevent this and therefore you are carrying guilt
- Forgiving God – for taking them from you so early and you may be mad/upset with Him wondering why He has allowed you to go through this and experience so much pain to the point where you feel that you are choking or even feel like you are dying yourself

During these times when you are experiencing this unforgiveness, you may keep away from the person who has offended you. Severing communication with them because you are so angry that just the mention of their name makes your blood boil raising negative emotions. Have you ever done this with God? Stayed away from Him, chosen not to communicate with Him, stayed away from church because you didn't want to hear anyone mention how good He is. Then quite possibly you might be holding some unforgiveness in your heart towards Him. You may even ask God what you have done that He has allowed you to suffer in so many ways. This may be the best time to seek Him, ask questions and He may reveal things that you never even knew.

Job 7 v 20-21 - If I have sinned, what have I done to you, you who see everything we do? Why have you made me your target? Have I become a burden to you? Why do you not pardon my offenses and forgive my sins? For I will soon lie down in the dust; you will search for me, but I will be no more. (NIV)

You might even share your situation with others who could actually justify your feelings towards the offender and delay the forgiving process. Looking at Job's story in the Bible, he would have been totally justified in his actions if he chose not to forgive God for taking his family. This is a man who lost everything in one day, his children and his entire livelihood. As we recall, God actually allowed this to happen to him and gave the devil authority to do so – as a test of his faith (now that's some serious testing). However, he continued to praise God throughout.

After losing all of this, Job 1 v 20–22 says *At this, Job got up and tore his robe and shaved his head. Then he fell to the ground in worship and said: "Naked I came from my mother's womb, and naked I will depart. The Lord gave and the Lord has taken away; may the name of the Lord be praised. In all this, Job did not sin by charging God with wrongdoing. (NIV)*

This was a major event in his life and he was heavily stricken with grief. Even after this, his health was also impacted, his wife told him to curse God and die yet he never gave up hope in Him.

Job's faith and love of God was so strong that nothing could stop him from praising and worshipping God throughout this situation. Job even asked God for forgiveness for any sins he may have committed that he wasn't aware of. We may not always know that we have offended someone or even committed a sin. But are you as faithful as Job? Just as we are meant to thank God, we should ask for his forgiveness and He will continually forgive us of our sins. Remember that what we may think is a small sin is still a sin.

As I've said, we may be the offenders and have to seek forgiveness from those that we have offended, possibly having to do a lot of work to regain their trust. Within Acts 9 the scripture focusses on forgiveness and the story of Saul. The disciples were in fear of him as he had killed and was seeking to kill all who were followers of Christ. God blinded Saul for three days and after this time he felt convicted. I can only assume that during those days he was able to reflect on his behaviour and the sins he had committed against God's people. God even sent his disciple Ananias to regain Saul's sight. It says that something like scales fell from his eyes and he could see again. When this happened, he was able to see the wrong that he had done and was filled with the Holy Spirt. From that day his attitude changed as well as his name. The disciples also saw the change and were able to forgive him. Now could you forgive someone you couldn't trust that had threatened to slay you and now you were to be walking by their side? Wouldn't you have some doubt in your mind that they could turn against you again? So, as well as forgiving those that have offended us, we need to seek forgiveness from those we may have offended also.

You may also have that unforgiveness towards God within you, but eventually when you realise that God is not at fault you need to ask for forgiveness for doubting Him. Even though you may have felt desperate during these times, He was there giving you the comfort throughout those grief stricken moments. He gives you the strength, courage and boldness to get through as well as to forgive yourself

How many times have you heard someone say 'I don't know how I made it through this situation and where I found the strength'? Well I can say that God is the one who carried you when you were weary and gave you the strength when you were weak. Admittedly, I have been angry with God on occasions, asking why He would allow me to experience such difficulties. Why He had forsaken me by taking people out of my life. Why He allowed me to endure such heartache to the point of becoming ill. I blamed Him for a lot of things, but eventually I felt ashamed and had to seek His forgiveness.

When I became a Christian, God forgave me of my sins and I forgot the former things I had done, however, there are still times I remember them. I am now a new creature in Christ with my walk starting on a blank sheet and the pages are filling up with my story. Some days aren't particularly great and I need to ask God for His forgiveness, for the heart to forgive others and most importantly for the courage to forgive myself. However, I am learning that it does become easier over time which is only due to the knowledge and wisdom that God has bestowed upon me.

Chapter 12

That Selah Moment!

M*eaning of Selah – Amplified Bible "Pause and think of that"* I believe we have all experienced moments where we have had to take stock of our lives and make necessary changes. These changes are normally for the good and generally hit us when we are mentally or emotionally exhausted. These are the times when we should stop what we are doing and reflect. A time to pause and think.

I have had several times throughout my life where I have done this and December 2015, in particular, is a time that I shall never forget. In fact, the whole year was very challenging for me. In September 2014, I was diagnosed with Type 2 Diabetes and had to start taking medication, on top of taking medication for high blood pressure. This was a time for me to come to terms with this new illness and try to understand it. Believe me, it wasn't easy to accept that this was happening to me. I started to blame myself for getting this disease. The smoking didn't really help and neither did my continual worrying about things. I had been feeling unwell for some time and couldn't work out what the problem was. I had been constantly feeling lethargic, literally struggling to get out of bed, and was also taking frequent time off work. After having blood tests, I finally received the call from my doctor with the diagnosis and was in total shock, feeling completely devastated. When I told my family, I recall my sister saying to me, it's not that bad and that it could be a lot worse. I know that she was trying to console me at the time and I never ignore the fact that there are worse situations that people experience. However, I bluntly told her it was easy for her to say as she was not the one having to take tablets to try and keep her alive.

Although I was glad to know what was making me feel so unwell, I still felt broken, angry, scared and confused. This was a life-threatening disease I had been diagnosed with and it needed to be managed. Also, with diabetes you need to try and keep your stress levels down. All this new information about diabetes was overwhelming. My daughter was dependent upon me to take care of her, so this couldn't be happening to me. I had to make the necessary changes to extend my life. My mind went into overdrive, I was so scared and feared not waking up in the morning with my daughter finding me dead and leaving her behind. Which may seem a little extreme to some but I couldn't control those thoughts and many nights I would go to sleep crying feeling lost and alone. I spoke to my mother who had been diagnosed 20 years earlier with it and realised she experienced the same emotions I was feeling. At the time when she told us we didn't realise how upsetting it was for her and what she was going through. It also made me realise that if she had made it this far and was in her 70's I could do the same, but only if I did the correct things to manage it. Even telling people was difficult as they start to judge, tell you what you can and can't do without even knowing the facts about the disease. I did, however, realise that all they were trying to do was help. At least I had mum who understood and could guide me.

One night I prayed so hard to God and asked Him to help me make those changes. The word *Jesus*! just flew out of my mouth. Not in a way that it had ever done before and the next morning I woke up and stopped smoking immediately and began eating healthier foods. Whilst trying to process this all and adjust, by the end of the year more issues started to arise. My daughter threw up a few challenges, which I honestly didn't know how to deal with. Her behaviour had changed significantly and I can only say that this was down to the issues she had been experiencing at school. In front of me was a child I hardly recognised and as much as I tried to support her and understand what she was going through, nothing seemed to work. I felt I had done all I could as a parent but had no control over what was going on with her. I felt desperate, unsupported and just didn't know what to do. All I can say is 2015 didn't start off very well and as the year progressed, more and more things kept coming which was definitely an attack by the enemy.

Ashamedly, I started smoking again to alleviate some of the stress, although it didn't make much of a difference. Certain days I could cope with whilst others were too overwhelming. I would go into work and my mind was not focussed on the job but on what was going on at home with my daughter. Many times I would end up in the ladies' toilets sobbing my heart out, just wanting to scream or walk out of the building and not come back. The Human Resources department was questioning my attendance and they were on the verge of taking me through a disciplinary process. My line managers were amazing and they could see I was going through a lot of stress. My character had changed dramatically and they managed to stop HR taking action and referred me to Occupational Health, where I was able to see a counsellor.

One weekend, in December 2015, I was being attacked from all corners by the enemy. On the Saturday evening my daughter threw up another curve ball which struck me in the pit of my stomach. I cried so hard and at one point I was literally curled up in a ball in my kitchen weeping inconsolably. Finding it difficult to sleep, I still arose on the Sunday morning and went to church. I knew it was the plan of the enemy for me not to attend as I had promised to sing as part of the Mission Service that is led by my mother. I remember standing on the altar and talking about the plans of the enemy and that he didn't want me to be there, but I refused to be defeated. I started to sing "Never Would Have Made It" by Marvin Sapp with tears streaming down my eyes. I was overwhelmed and started declaring victory over my life commanding the enemy to stay away from my family. I left church feeling energised, but by the evening things started to spiral out of control again. I couldn't cope and felt that I had failed in my duty as a parent so decided to send my daughter to my mother's for a few days.

She was unapologetic and was acting very cold at that point and I was feeling so hurt. This could not be my baby in front of me acting in the way she was. Although I understood she was going through a difficult time at school, I didn't recognise at that point how deep the hurt was and acting out in such a manner was the only way she could express herself. After returning from mum's, later that evening I jumped into my car and just drove having no idea where I was going. I felt so trapped and just needed to escape. I needed to clear my head, but even the drive made no difference. Eventually I returned home, knocked back a couple glasses of Jack Daniels which I thought would numb the pain and went to bed. The following morning, I awoke as usual to go to work as I refused to be defeated by my circumstances.

During that week, more things came to attack me, with a sudden death within the family which immediately changed the course of things. There was also an additional situation that arose within the family that my siblings didn't want to tell me about as they didn't believe I could handle any more bad news. It was a surreal experience but one that I will never forget. However, these events really opened my eyes to the things that are truly important which was health and family. I noticed my attitude changed significantly and my relationship with my daughter had improved.

I no longer had time for insignificant things such as gossip about others or anything that didn't have any direct consequence to my immediate family's lives or my own. I would not allow my mind to be saturated with minor things and therefore would shut down conversations speedily. Even if it meant offending people along the way, but at that point I simply didn't care. I was in a position to say what my mind should absorb and a lot of the things we take on are pollutants. We should be free and peaceful beings. This was something I had been yearning for and I had reached a place where I didn't want any drama in my life. I have learnt that if we feed these things then they will grow substantially until we start to be consumed by them.

I was also able to release what was going on in my life with the counsellor and was given a place of safety to vent my frustrations, fears and shed many tears. Even if it was just for one hour a week. It is so difficult to gain clarity within your mind when so many obstacles and battles are placed in front of you. I simply didn't know what to do to regain control over my life or my mind. Although throughout I never gave up hope in God. I believe that by having a relationship with Him and knowing that He had brought me through previous struggles, I still had faith that He would continue to do the same.

I made so many adjustments in my life the following year. Removing the strongholds that had been holding me captive, refusing to be taken for granted and allowing myself to grow. I refused to allow toxicity to eat away at me and stunt my growth. Although it had taken me a long time to realise what things were depleting me, it was the catalyst I needed to bring me to where I am today. Since making these changes, admittedly I have a more positive attitude within myself, have become more focussed and closer to achieving my goals and the purpose God has for me.

The enemy knew that if I was being attacked then my health would be impacted further, but I was determined that he would not succeed. I refused to allow him to be ruler over my life and declared that "I shall live and not die". I am still enduring battles but now choose which ones to give my energy to.

We should not give the enemy control over our lives, but make a declaration that God is our strength, rock and stronghold and that we are not victims but victorious. In the storms we should pause, remain calm and just wait for them to pass, because they will.

Selah!

Chapter 13

It's Not the End, it's a New Beginning!

Consider, when something comes to an end, what do we tend to do? Do we panic for fear of the unknown? We are now put in a position where we may need to put a new vision in place and sometimes we have no vision at all. A situation such as redundancy, relationship breakdowns or death could prevent you from looking forward as you simply can't see a future without this person or thing in your life. We are not always prepared and don't adjust well to change. However, we need to recognise that although this may be the end of that situation and that chapter in our life has ended, it is not the end for us. Even when we depart from this world, we still have eternal life, but whilst we are alive on this Earth this may be the beginning of a new chapter in our lives.

One thing that could be preventing us from moving onto the next chapter for example could be us holding onto unforgiveness. This can be very toxic to our soul/spirit and can stunt our growth. Therefore, we need to look at the things that need to come to an end, especially if it is not allowing us to be productive and is holding us captive. How do we do this and allow ourselves to move forward? I believe you will need to take a closer inspection of yourself identifying what needs to be brought to an end which will allow you to start that new chapter in your life. Ask God to show you how to release yourself from the bondage. The topic of Forgiveness has already been covered in the book but we need to continually look at any areas where we are holding onto unforgiveness. We need to be completely honest with ourselves and ask God to help us in those areas. Until you truly release that hurt, anger, resentment, and frustration and have a free spirit, then you cannot be released to move forward.

One night whilst preparing for one of our prayer meetings at work, the words "it's not the end, it's a new beginning!" came to my mind. I started to delve a little deeper as to the message God wanted me to deliver and what it could mean. Isaiah 43 v 18–19 was pressed into my spirit. The group hadn't met for some time and I was keen to see where God was leading me with this. I put my thoughts across at the meeting as to what this meant to me and we then started to discuss it further.

Isaiah 43 v 18–19 Forget the former things; do not dwell on the past. See I am doing a new thing! Now it springs up; do you not perceive it? I am making a way in the wilderness and streams in the wasteland. (NIV)

The scripture says to forget the former things and to look forward, even if we cannot see what is ahead of us, and if you read further on it says that God will make a way in the wilderness (those times when we are feeling lost).

We discussed this scripture as well as hitting on the subject of forgiveness within the meeting. One of the ladies said that she was experiencing a situation where people had started rumours about her. She felt that they were defaming her character and it was obvious to us that this was causing her a great deal of upset. She said that she had forgiven them but this clearly wasn't the case and she was allowing the situation to overwhelm her. We suggested that she start to create that new beginning by releasing that hurt, anger and resentment towards the person, which would allow her to find inner peace. If she believed that she had done nothing wrong, she simply had nothing to prove to anyone else but God as He knows her heart. There were suggestions for her to remove the negative energy that was overwhelming her and to fix her eyes on God and He will fix the rest.

I had recently experienced a situation where there was unforgiveness in my heart towards my daughter's father and I had to write down my feelings, be honest with myself and say what I was forgiving him for. Although I also had to forgive myself and be accountable for what I had done. A few days later, after writing these things down, the words "flush them away" fell into my spirit. So I immediately got up with the screwed up piece of paper in my hand and flushed it away. Whenever I have had any negative thoughts arise towards him I simply say, "I flushed them away", shifting my thoughts onto something more positive. I suggested that this lady should do the same towards this person that had hurt her.

We finished the prayer meeting and the following morning she sent me a message saying "My Lord has done it for me. I just had a wonderful encounter with my Lord and Saviour". All I could say was "God is amazing and is always on time". The new chapter in her life could now begin. Praise God!

One of my friends summarised the walk of faith with God and dealing with closing doors behind you and the uncertainty of life in just a few words by saying **"All you need to do is focus on the step and God will build the staircase."**

A wise monkey named Rafiki from the *Lion King* also summed it up when he told Simba to "look beyond what you see".

Therefore, we should be open to new experiences such as:

- stepping out of our comfort zone (not being afraid to move forward and breaking the mould)
- believing in yourself more (trusting in your decisions, even if you cannot see the end)
- tapping into your talents/gifts that God has given you
- meeting new people (surrounding yourself with positive people that will encourage and not discourage you)

Never did I believe that I, Karen Holder, would be writing a book. I always had the thoughts in my head, but always brushed them aside, pushing them to the back of my mind. I would say it was just a dream that was out of my reach. But here I am in my 40's doing just that. I have many other talents that I have sat upon and I have now started to believe in myself. There were a lot of things in my life that hindered me and most of them were caused by my own self-doubt. I believed these things were not attainable and I spent too much time worrying about what other people might think of me. By spending so much time worrying I was delaying my growth. I am now more open to trying out new things. Removing the negative people and connecting myself with the right people who believe in my vision has also given me the kick start that I needed.

I have now created that new chapter in my life and truly believe that I am no longer bound by my past. I have broken free from that place of captivity. I understood that if I continued with my old way of thinking and not bringing certain situations to a close, then the outcome would continually be the same and my progression hindered. However, by taking authority over my life, I have been able to re-write my future.

Now ask yourself the following questions;

- Am I ready to give up the past?
- What do I want the next chapter to be in my life?
- Do I want a new beginning?
- What steps do I need to take to create it?

Part 3

Revelation

Chapter 14

Reality

A re you living an illusion or reality?

As much as I believe in God and say that I am Christian, my life is not always a true reflection of what a Christian life should be. The reality is that sometimes I mess up big time but I try to be honest with myself when I do. Other times I may just paint a picture to make me look good or to make people believe that I am coping, creating an illusion. Admitting that to myself, brings me back to reality and the truth. No matter who we pretend to be, God knows the truth and therefore we cannot hide from Him. People may perceive us in many different ways, but only God knows who we truly are and can see behind the façade.

Someone may ask you how you are doing. Most times we paint a picture that all is going well and we have everything under control. Sometimes we may believe within ourselves that it is the truth but it can be far from the reality. Some people are fortunate enough to have a confidante but even then we may withhold certain details and not reveal everything that is going on with us at the time. Maybe we don't want to burden people with our issues so the easiest response is to say, "I'm okay". But are we really?

We have a vision of how we would like things to be but inwardly we are suffering. By not being honest at least with ourselves, maintaining that façade can be extremely exhausting. I have had to be honest with myself coming to the realisation that my life isn't perfect and when my circumstances have become overwhelming I may start to live a life of denial. Why would that be? Is it because I want to escape into a fantasy world as I don't want to accept what is going on?

Here are a couple of examples of what I mean by this. As you know I was diagnosed with Type 2 Diabetes which was and still is, if I'm being perfectly honest, at times difficult for me to accept. On top of this I also have high blood pressure and I am taking medication for both of these ailments. I know that major adjustments have to be made to my lifestyle/habits, i.e. losing weight, eating healthier, exercising more, and quitting smoking, and if I don't make these adjustments things will obviously get worse as Diabetes is a progressive disease which needs to be controlled. It scares me that I may not be around to see my daughter grow into an adult. I will miss out on many important moments in her life and she will not have the memory of her mother sharing these moments with her. When I go to bed at night, I pray that God will allow me to wake up and spend another day with her and each day I am grateful that he has given me that day. That is the reality, and although I have lost weight (gradually I might add), my illusion is that by eating chocolate, continuing to smoke (although believe me I do want to quit) and taking part in sporadic exercise, I am denying I have this condition. I have been trying to live a normal life therefore pretending to people that I am okay. Admitting to people I have these illnesses, in particular Diabetes, was difficult at first but I just want to be like my friends, family and colleagues who don't have to watch what they eat; I want to not feel guilty if I eat chocolate, a sausage or some chips and I want to do so without people judging me. Sometimes I feel so low about it and want to cry my eyes out and tell people exactly how I feel at times, but then I don't just because I would prefer to give the illusion that all is well and don't want to burden anyone with my issues.

Attending appointments with a dietician, getting eye tests, regular blood tests, and blood pressure monitoring to ensure I am managing are all reminders that bring me to reality like a wakeup call. Many times when I have to collect my prescription from the chemist, I stand at the counter with tears in my eyes, but shake it off and carry on. There are nights and mornings when I am in floods of tears being face to face with the medication that is keeping me alive and I really do feel alone.

A second example is I have a problem with my finances with a fairly large credit card debt that I am keeping on top of, however, I am struggling to get released from it. This causes me stress at times and I try to live within a budget but things become difficult at times. With my conditions my stress levels should be kept to a minimum. As long as I have a job, then I should be okay, but if that disappears, I don't know how I would actually manage. Although being fully aware of the debt, sometimes I still purchase things that I know I shouldn't and start to feel guilty for a while but tell myself I can manage. That is the illusion, because I am not really managing. The reality is that I need to stop making excuses, otherwise things will get worse. I need to focus on paying off these debts, living within my means and seek some financial advice.

Are you pretending that you are happy in relationships when in actual fact they are tearing you down, breaking you? Are you experiencing abuse, verbal or physical? Are you believing that this person's behaviour towards you is a sign of love and that they do this because you are a bad person and you deserve it? Are you creating an image to the world that you are in a good place but you really want to escape and don't know how to? Or even wondering who you can confide in? You may be feeling lost, rejected, confused and totally isolated, yet smiling, telling everyone all is well. You believe that you can handle it and cover up the bruises but they are silently taking their toll on you.

I was hit by a partner when I was in my teens, only once I might add. I am not making excuses for him but I don't believe he was in his right state of mind at the time. Sad to say I think he was drug-fuelled. We never got back together but I had forgiven him for his behaviour. Admittedly, I have also been abusive towards a partner and I know that I was in a state of confusion; I had no control over my emotions. I was so angry as my trust had been abused and jealousy raised its ugly head. There he was telling me about this person who had taken my place temporarily whilst we were on a break. All I could imagine was that person touching him, showing him affection and my heart was being crushed with every word he spoke. He had put me on a pedestal and then swiftly kicked it from underneath me. I totally lost control and was throwing punches and screaming at him believing that he had ruined my life. Fortunately, he never retaliated in any way but the situation could have been different if he had. My behaviour was wrong and my illusion was that I loved him so much that I wanted him to understand how I was feeling. However, the reality was I was just making excuses to justify my actions as I should never have raised my hand to him at all. The reality was that these men could not have truly appreciated or valued me enough to treat me in the way that they did.

I have witnessed a few people suffer at the hands of domestic violence and it really hurts to watch especially with some of them suffering for many years. There was nothing that I could say to make them leave, even though their body was often covered in bruises and they started to become very withdrawn and so different from their former self. One of my school friends, who I lost contact with over time, used to have many guys beating on her to the point where her ribs were broken, but she declared that she loved them. I thought this girl had everything, a lovely home and both her mum and stepdad were amazing. She always had the latest clothes, technology, went on family holidays and always seemed to have it together, so I couldn't understand why she would allow herself to be treated in this way. She eventually became a target for boys and men and would also drink heavily as well as experiment with different drugs.

I remember seeing her at a party one evening where her partner had her bent over a wall. I went over and asked what was going on and his response was she was drunk and embarrassed him in the party so he was now going to take her home. I tried to calm them down and my friend was highly intoxicated. We spoke for a little while where I agreed that he should bring her home and as I walked away, I could hear her cursing at him. I didn't have her number but the next day I called her mum to see if she was alright. The first thing her mother said to me was, "were they fighting?" When I said *no*, her response was, "that makes a change". That seemed to be the norm for her but maybe she created an illusion by drinking and taking drugs to numb some secret emotional pain, covering up the hurt she was feeling inside. She couldn't see things clearly, but the reality was she didn't deserve to be treated that way. No one does. I pray that she has recognised her worth and found someone who truly loves her.

I am not trying to skirt over this issue, but domestic violence is a very serious topic that many people endure. They may believe their partner's behaviour is a way of expressing love when in reality it is a way of exercising control over a being as they are unable to control their own lives. How far will you allow it to go before you are willing to face reality and know that it is time to get out?

I am not suggesting that I am an expert in this subject, but generally it is fear that makes someone stay with an abusive partner. Fear of speaking up. Fear of retaliation. Fear of being alone. Fear that if they leave then people will judge them. Fear of not knowing where to go. Fear of not being able to start again. Fear of admitting to others that they have chosen the wrong person.

Even though we may try to hide our issues from others, deep down we know the reality. We know the decisions we make or the circumstances we find ourselves in are not right for us and therefore believe that creating an illusion to others is easier. The life that we are living is so far from the truth and we then become caught in a web of deceit. But all we are doing is deceiving ourselves. Isn't it better to acknowledge the truth and try to change those circumstances? The reality is that we may be able to hide from others but God is fully aware of what we are struggling with and we cannot run away from Him. Recognise that seeking counsel from God and having a relationship with Him you can remove the mask, speak the truth without being judged and He, in turn, will help you to be the discover the real you.

You may not have experienced any of the issues I have mentioned above, but you may want to consider what illusion you are creating for yourself or others and whether you are now willing to face the reality.

Chapter 15

The Shuffle of Life!

I see so many people going through situations that many others might not have been able to endure, and quite frankly I would have given up. I have said that so many times myself when things have become too much for me to bear. "Oh, I give up!" But in actual fact I don't and somehow find the strength and determination to get through. Although admittedly this is through God's power and might, not my own. I have to hand all the power over to Him when I don't have the strength to do it myself and as soon as I do there is a peace and calm that takes over. My perspective of the situation turns around completely and if I ever find myself in difficult circumstances, I take comfort in the fact that I can overcome them again, even if it takes longer than I would like.

For example, one particular evening upon my return from work, I noticed an old lady shuffling along at the station who I can only assume was connecting from one underground line to another. I am uncertain as to which platform she had come from but at the pace she was moving it had probably taken her some time to get there. Commuters were rushing past to get home from their day at the office, myself included. As I walked past her, I couldn't help but look back and watch her continue to shuffle along at a snail's pace. She would have had at least two escalators to ascend before she even got to the platform and if she was heading for the exit then that would be an additional set of escalators. There she was walking unaided and all alone. She was slightly arched over and her eyes were directed towards her feet as she continued moving along. As I reached the top of the escalator, I looked back again and she hadn't even reached the first step which was probably ten metres away. Now you may ask why I didn't stop to help her and to be honest I don't know why, but I was transfixed by the image of this old lady. I think I was so wrapped up in things that were going on in my life at the time that I failed to offer my assistance. It was the period in 2015 when things weren't going too good for me and I was completely overwhelmed feeling emotionally, physically and mentally exhausted, and found myself simply going through the motions of life.

Watching this old lady from the top of the escalator, it was as if a light came on and I personally believe that God placed her there for a reason. Because I remember thinking, this lady no matter how long it took her to reach her final destination, is sliding one foot in front of the other to get there. Just shuffling along, even though it may be a long and hard journey for her, it was one that she was determined to make on her own. She planned to conquer the obstacles before her. Though they may have seemed overwhelming, she was willing to overcome them even if it took her longer than other people. She may have had an appointment knowing that she would have to set out a little earlier to get there but she would arrive on time. It showed me that although I was going through my difficulties, all I had to do was rise and put one foot in front of the other and I would reach my chosen destination. Even if I was tired, my strength would come through every step I made by simply moving forward, focusing on what was ahead and not giving up. Even if all I did was shuffle along, I could make it and reach my destination at the right time.

God really shows up at the times I need Him and I remember being directed to the scriptures below whilst going through a very low time. I was sat at home alone watching Joyce Meyers on one of the God channels when she referenced the following scriptures.

2 Corinthians 4 v 8-9 We are hedged in (pressed) on every side (troubled and oppressed in every way) but not cramped or crushed; we suffer embarrassments and are perplexed and unable to find a way out, but not driven to despair. We are pursued (persecuted and hard driven) but not deserted (to stand alone): we are struck down to the ground, but never struck out and destroyed. (AMP)

2 Corinthians 4 16–17 Therefore we do not become discouraged (utterly spiritless, exhausted and wearied out through fear). Though our outer man is (progressively) decaying and wasting away, yet our inner self is being (progressively) renewed day after day.

For our light, momentary affliction (this slight distress of the passing hour) is ever more and more abundantly preparing and producing and achieving for us an everlasting weight of glory (beyond all measure, excessively surpassing all comparisons and all calculations, a vast and transcendent glory and blessedness never to cease).

Since we consider and look not to the things that are seen but to the things that are unseen; for the things that are visible are temporal (brief and fleeting) but the things that are invisible are deathless and everlasting. (AMP)

It was a New Year and although the beginning of most New Year's tended to start off good, after a few days, I would start to feel fed up probably because I hadn't actually let go of things in the past. I now have a name for these times and call them 'seasonal moments'. I would often remove myself from people, preferring to be alone, and throw myself a pity party. On this occasion, I felt totally alone. My ex and I would often alternate the Christmas and New Year holidays, and my daughter was spending this time with her dad. In my head I was thinking this should have been a time for us to be celebrating together but here I was in my flat alone again. I had no one to celebrate with and all I could think of was him being around someone else and our daughter being with them. As much as I tried to accept it, it was difficult especially when she would come home with gifts that she received from them. I often had to put my feelings aside for her sake and pretend I was delighted with the gifts she got when all I wanted to do was throw them in the bin.

When the programme I was watching finished, I went to bed not feeling any different, but throughout the night I experienced the following dream that filled me with a new song. In the dream I was asleep in my bed and when I awoke I said, "Where are you Jesus?" I saw a bright light under my bed and rolled over and looked underneath. There were things in the way preventing me from reaching the light so I then started to move all the clutter that was almost blocking it. I even found a Telly Tubby that I picked up, threw to the side and said, "You are not God." I continued to search and the light still continued to shine under the bed. Suddenly, my attention was drawn away and I looked to the bedroom door and saw a troop of what I can only call demons marching past my room that made their way out of the front door. I awoke quickly from my dream and sat up reflecting and that spirit of heaviness had left me and the lightness entered in as the enemy departed. Immediately the words *Jesus you are my friend* fell into my spirit and I then started to write a song based on this, which you will find in the **Chapter 16 'A New Song'**. I felt such an inner peace, which was beyond all understanding. Eventually, I went back to bed and in the early hours of the morning I contacted the church leader and asked if I could give my testimony at church that day. I was so charged up and wanted to tell everyone about my deliverance. I shared the events of that night, even the bit about the Telly Tubby, and sang my new song. I was totally uplifted and at one point whilst singing the song, I turned around and two of the worship leaders were behind me doing backing vocals and the congregation was also singing along to it. For a time after that, members of the congregation were actually making requests for me to sing the song. Jesus is the only friend that walks with us constantly through all of our situations and battles.

I overcame this situation and the one in 2015, and in summary the scripture tells us that our circumstances are temporal. Although we may be hard pressed, boxed in to the point of feeling crushed, we do not stand alone. With each trial that we face our inner spirit is being strengthened every day. We just need to understand that even whilst being at a point where we feel there is no hope, God's everlasting light shines through us. God's light will help us on the way and we should be encouraged that the situation will pass.

Isaiah 40 v31 But those who wait for the Lord [who expect, look for, and hope in Him] Will gain new strength and renew their power; They will lift up their wings [and rise up close to God] like eagles [rising toward the sun]; They will run and not become weary, They will walk and not grow tired. (AMP)

Keep looking forward and do not get overwhelmed by the journey ahead of you wondering how you will make it. Even if it feels that you are just shuffling and going nowhere fast, God is constantly at your side and will renew your strength enabling you to soar with wings like eagles.

Chapter 16

A New Song

As I mentioned previously, I have awoken many times in the middle of the night when God has filled me with new songs/poems, and within this chapter I would like to share some of these with you. These are songs that have helped to inspire me as well as others and I pray that one of them will help you in the same way. At the times they were written, I was at different places in my life, so some of these were created when I needed answers to questions, when I was feeling low and also when I wanted to express my thanks and love for God for all the wonderful things He had done for me and give glory and honour to His name.

As you read through the Bible, you will note that Abraham and Isaac experienced similar events in their lives even though they were a generation apart. Both the father and son had wives who were barren. Sometimes we face that barrenness, but just as God turned their situations around and allowed their wives to deliver children, He can also deliver you out of situations where you believe that the odds are against you. Basically, I am saying that I know that I am not the only person to endure difficulties in my life and therefore I believe that God did not want me to keep these to myself but to use them in a way that His children would be encouraged.

Sing to the Lord a new song (inspired by Psalm 96)

Chorus
Sing to the Lord a new song
Sing to the Lord all the Earth
Sing to the Lord bless His Holy Name
Show forth His salvation from day to day

Declare His glory among the nations
His marvellous works among all men
For great is Lord and greatly to be praised
We need to exalt Him and magnify His Name

(Repeat Chorus)

Give to the Lord the glory due His Name
Worship the Lord in Holiness
Say among the nations that the Lord He reigns
And we need to exalt Him and magnify His Name

Is it you Lord?

Who is it that calls out my name and tells me things will never be the same? Is it you Lord?
Who is it that tells me to come into the light as better doth shine? Is it you Lord?

Yes it is you Lord that keeps my feet from stumbling and hears my incoherent mumbling.
Who speaks to me in the dead of night, telling me, "my child, everything will be alright".

I long to hear your voice to give me direction and cannot get by without our connection.
You are the wind beneath my wings, giving me the strength to continue soaring.
Flying past all adversity and my spirit you are constantly restoring.

Yes it is you Lord who comforts me through the pain.
Yes it is you Lord that enlarges my domain.
Yes it is you Lord that I seek through necessity.

Yes it is you Lord that continually blesses me.

Yes, it really is you Lord!

Where Would I Be?

Where would I be – where would I go?
If you weren't there – there to show?
Lord I know You are with me – every step of the way
Even though I can't see You, I know you are near

You lift me up when no one else can, You are mightier than any man
I honour You and magnify Your Name, with You Father I am no longer ashamed
You forgive me when no one else will, You overlook my faults and teach me to be still
I appreciate all that You have done, and know that with You all my battles are won

Father You have rescued me and accepted me as family
I am truly honoured and grateful You chose me, without you Father where would I be?

When I lay down on my bed at night and think about all the tears I cried
You're always there to see me through, that's why Father I put all my trust in You
You dry those tears and shelter me from harm, You turn the storms to a safe and gentle calm
You lift me up and I praise and honour You, without You Father what would I do?

I Just Can't Make It On My Own

Show me the way my Father, Make the paths clear for me
Open my eyes to my future. Father help me!
Give me the understanding, make my life brand new
Show me the way my Father, so I can get closer to You

I just can't make it on my own – I need You
I just can't make it on my own – rescue me Lord

I'm just a humble servant, wanting to honour You
Father I need your guidance, so you can help me through
I know that I sin and falter, but You are not far behind
You show me your love and mercy, how can You be so kind

I just can't make it on my own – I need You
I just can't make it on my own – rescue me Lord

When all your love was taken for granted and You sent Jesus to set us free
He gave up his life for us, at Calvary
Father I need your guidance, Father help me see
Please let me find the way Lord, so I can be with Thee

I just can't make it on my own – I need You
I just can't make it on my own – rescue me Lord

Why Do You Run Away From Me?

Why do you run away from me, when all I want to do is help?
Why do you run away from me, believing you should do everything
by yourself?
You say that you truly believe, but yet you distance yourself from me
You say that you will put your trust in me, but then turn around and flee

You know that I am the rock of your salvation and will never leave you to stand alone
I am the one that comforts you and will give you the strength to soldier on
Therefore, do not be discouraged or be afraid, I am not one to fear
I know the plans I have for you and they are not ones of despair

Just surrender all to me, your burdens I shall carry
Freely give your heart to me and I will ensure you will not tarry
You have been in the same place for too long and it's time to take you out
I will give you a new song filled with joy and peace and let everyone hear your shout

So place your hands firmly in mine and I will pull you through
Place your trust solely in me and see my works reign true
You mean everything to me so do not be ashamed
You are a diadem in my hand, a part of the royal priesthood I have named

Reach out your hand to touch my garment I am not far away
I shall not turn away from you, for I am here to stay

Take These Burdens

Lord just take these burdens from me, even for a night
Hide them in a box somewhere so I can sleep tonight
I know that you are always with me and give me strength to fight
Lord just take these burdens for a night

No Matter What the Situation

No matter what the situation
He'll make the sun shine through the rain
No matter what the circumstance
He'll make you smile again.

Jesus You Are My Friend

Jesus, Jesus you are my friend (repeat 4 times)
You mean the world to me, you died on Calvary
With you I am set free, Jesus you're my friend
Put all my faith in you, only you can see me through
With you I am renewed, Jesus you're my friend

God will also fill you with a new song if you allow him to come into your life.

Chapter 17

Drawn to Likeminded People

I have found that over the years God has removed certain people from my life and led me towards people that are bringing positivity into my life. I believe that people have always been drawn towards me for encouragement, even if for a short time.

As I have grown, I have tried to be as direct and honest with people as I possibly could. This could be a good thing but sometimes not so. There are times when I have had to stifle my words using the technique of humility that the Father has blessed me with by not saying anything at all and trying to protect them. Sometimes I wish that I didn't have to as I believe that certain people need to be told how their behaviour may come across as offensive or their actions may have affected people in a negative way. I am fairly transparent, so even if I don't say anything my actions towards them will definitely speak louder than words.

I have been told so many times by people how they admire me; that I am strong and have a quality of a leader. They have said I encouraged them along the way and have also received numerous compliments on my appearance. I remember one particular friend changing the way they dressed to look like me and to be honest with you I found this a little scary. One day I turned up at her house as we were going for a night out and was deeply shocked to find a reflection of myself standing in front of me. Sometimes, I don't feel strong and wonder what positive things they are seeing when I can't always see them in myself. I don't always know what I have done to make them feel this way towards me apart from being me. Some days I just get up, get dressed and try and look like I have it all together when in actual fact I am falling apart. Maybe that's what they see in me, the fact that I persist and continue to walk with my head held high no matter what the circumstances.

People can be in your life for a reason, season or a lifetime and those that are meant to stay will. Others might just be there for me to help them in their healing process or for them to afford the same to me. Just like the old lady I mentioned in the **Chapter 15 'Shuffle of Life'** who I saw at the train station, she taught me a valuable life lesson. There was a reason for our paths crossing even though we never exchanged any words.

Now when I say we are drawn towards likeminded people, this is not always a positive thing but could be to our detriment. If you are surrounded by people who suffer from drug addictions the likelihood is that you could turn out the same. Your initial intention might have been to go and help them but eventually you may get drawn in and their bad habits could become yours. A possible way to have turned that situation around is to remove them out of that circle and bring them into a circle of people who have a different perspective. However, the whole point of this chapter is for you to set yourself around people that will edify you, motivate you, build you up and help you to reach your full potential.

I have had to do some culling of friendships/relationships over the years. I wouldn't say I have an army of friends but the ones that I do have in my life I have chosen wisely. I don't just accept anyone into my life or circle without getting an understanding of who they are and my spirit has to take to them. I had one friend that I used to hang out with quite a lot, but over the years the relationship changed and we gradually stopped spending as much time together. I understood that the friendship had run its course and had taken on a different dynamic. I would still invite them out to events, but after a while I realised it was not always reciprocated so eventually I gave up and accepted it for what it was. However, there are times that I see them and they always end the conversation with 'we must meet up'. I'm not quite sure why they say that but yet make no effort to arrange anything. And the conversations we have when we happen to bump into one another always feels strained and not genuine to me. So I don't see the point in pursuing it if I don't feel comfortable. I understand that life can get in the way but I do have an amazing set of friends that even if we haven't seen or spoken to one another for a long time, we value and appreciate one another and just carry on from where we left off. I don't see the need in begging people to be around me if they don't want to be a part of my life. It is important to me to have people around that I can be honest and free with and they can feel the same with me. Having been burnt too many times by people, I exercise extreme caution. However, I do give people the benefit of the doubt but also give them enough rope to hang themselves.

At my previous job a number of colleagues and myself formed a Prayer & Praise group where we would meet once a week during lunch. The main focus of the group was for us to fellowship with one another, discuss our understanding of the Scriptures and talk about the trials we faced as Christians. We would go in there feeling hungry but leave the meetings filled with the Word and the Holy Spirit. We were all in search of the same thing which was developing and maintaining a better relationship with God. Sometimes it would be challenging for us all to be present every week owing to work commitments but I can proudly say that it ran for a number of years which shows there was a need for it. However, if we did not get a chance to meet on the designated day, we still found an opportunity to talk in the kitchen or at our desks. This gave us an opportunity to discuss any challenges we may have been facing. As well as uplifting and encouraging one another through battles, it also aided us in continually trusting and putting our faith in God. There were people who attended and left over the years, having either left or moved to different parts of the organisation. However, I truly believe that they were edified during that time and managed to receive the help and comfort they needed during their journey. Unfortunately, I have now left the organisation but received a great deal of support and upliftment during those times. The other members of the group had also been moved to different locations following a restructure, however, we have created a WhatsApp group where we still keep in touch to share the word of God and encourage one another on our journeys. We were drawn to one another to create this group and believed in it so much that we continue to keep it going.

If you are a Christian and attend church, you may also find that not everyone will act or think like you and you may have differing opinions. Some may have their own interpretations of scriptures that they try to force upon you and tell you what it means to be a Christian. I don't always take everyone's word as bond and will ask God for discernment and direction. There are times when I have been annoyed with church members when they have told me what they believe I should be doing. Some would speak into my life and not really know me as an individual. Oftentimes this may have been said in love but I felt that they were passing judgement upon me and I wanted to tell them to keep their opinions to themselves. Some people may say they know you, but do they really? Sometimes we only show them little bits of us, covering up our iniquities as we are afraid to be vulnerable for fear of being judged. However, we can be completely free with God as He knows our inner thoughts. I try to be as honest with people as I can regarding my struggles as a Christian woman, but there are many that still continue to live a façade.

Sometimes we can find ourselves surrounded by people that are not lifting us up emotionally, mentally or spiritually. These are the kind of people that are not our advocates but only there to prevent us from meeting our full potential. I wonder if by attracting these people it could just be an inner reflection of what we feel about ourselves. Because we do not view ourselves as valuable, we therefore limit our growth, depleting any hope that we have to find that inner joy and peace. So until we see the value that is within us, these people will just confirm the negative image we have of ourselves.

When I first started to attend my local church, there were certain people I was instantly drawn to. These were people that I believed I could learn something from. Although we built up a relationship, mainly within the church, we never actually met up or spoke to one another outside. However, there was one particular lady that I used to just pass pleasantries with, not striking up much of a conversation. Admittedly, I had some reservations about her as I couldn't quite work her out and found it somewhat difficult to maintain conversation with her. It always felt a little awkward. In 2003, I started a new job and this same person was employed there on a temporary contract. Little did I know, that I was the project she was working on. We started to talk in the kitchen as we both recognised one another from church and eventually started going for lunch time walks together. On these walks we would talk about life in general and God. At that time, I was uncertain about my journey and I asked her where God was and how she knew He existed. She just pointed upwards and encouraged me to read the Bible more. The only time I would really pick up the Bible was at church and when I did read it the words didn't make any sense or resonate with me. We started to build a friendship and sometimes she would invite herself to my home after church for Sunday dinner. I never found her intrusive at all, but just accepted her and we would sit and talk for ages. Even though I said I was a bit sceptical of her in the beginning, my relationship with her actually drew me closer to God.

Proverbs 27 v 17 As Iron sharpens Iron, so one person sharpens another. (NIV)

Hebrews 4v12 For the word of God is quick, and powerful, and sharper than any two-edged sword, piercing even to the dividing asunder of soul and spirit, and of the joints and marrow, and is a discerner of the thoughts and intents of the heart. (KJV)

God recognised that my relationship with Him was dull and the other members of the church were not able to fully reach me as maybe I only wanted to know Him on a superficial level. However, He sent along another person that I least expected to get along with to bring me closer to Him. This enabled me to work out the purpose He had for me and to become sharper in His word. For that I am truly grateful.

In 2017, I met a young lady that was rather cynical towards Christian women and the church. I later found out that she had grown up in a church environment and did not have a good experience with some of the members. We had not known one another for a long period but we got along very well spending hours on the phone and just being very open. We met at a workshop and she said that she had been drawn to me and actually sent me a message expressing how she felt which I have decided to share with you. It read *"You are one of the most open Christian women that I have come across. People need to know how amazing you are and your book will provide just that. One of the reasons I walked away from church is because I felt that women put a huge front on. They weren't real with themselves and preached to others to change when they needed to change 'self' first. It really annoyed me. Thank God you are real. That's what makes me feel safe to open up to you – so thank you."*

Unfortunately, we no longer remain in contact but for the time we spent together, I believe that we were both able to help and encourage one another during that brief period and she definitely provided me with the confidence to write this book. In particular, to show that Christian's do have flaws and we are not all perfect. People may be in your life for a season, reason or a lifetime and you may be drawn to them without knowing the purpose or the length of time that they will be there. This young lady was in my life for a season and when we spoke, it was as if we knew one another for years. Although the communication ended abruptly, maybe that was how it was intended and the purpose and plans of God had been fulfilled. We do not always acknowledge the impact we can have on a person or they can have on us. Whether it be a positive or negative impact there is always a valuable lesson to learn for both parties. Therefore, we should embrace them, not compromising who we are for fear of not knowing whether it will end. But it might also create that new chapter in our life that was required.

I do believe that we should be guarded but not completely closed to receive people into our lives that will edify us. It is not always about image and how a person looks. These people don't have to be wearing the latest designer clothes, always be looking good or have a particular status to enable them to have a positive impact in your life. Admittedly, I have at times passed judgement on people and they have gotten on my last nerve, but over time and by letting my guard down, I have formed many good relationships with those same people. Some of them have also helped me on my Christian walk and I have been friends with them for many years and know they will be there for a lifetime. These people have supported me through my trials and been there when I least expected them. So, I am thankful that I shed my ignorance allowing them to enter in.

What kind of people are you surrounding yourself with? Are they people who add or subtract from your life?

Chapter 18

Come into the Light

J eremiah 29 v 11 "For I know the plans I have for you," declares the Lord, "plans to prosper you and not to harm you, plans to give you hope and a future." (NIV)

From a young age, I believe that God was calling me. You may remember my mention of evangelising to school friends in the Introduction. I did this in the playground with Bible in hand. When we were younger and living in Shepherd's Bush, my siblings and I would attend Sunday school. However, I don't recall much of what was being said and was always waiting for it to end. This would be an opportunity to get sweets or biscuits from the Sunday school teacher and I could then leave there smiling. One day she didn't give out anything. I thought she was joking and having waited around for a while with my siblings I left feeling greatly disappointed. Sundays were often very busy and in the evening we would attend a Jehovah's Witness church with mum. There were always lots of people in attendance and some of the children that lived locally or attended my school would be there also. When we moved, after a while our attendance at church stopped. Mum wasn't saved at that point but she would be visited regularly by Jehovah's Witness representatives. I remember a lady named Jane and her husband would often come and sit down to minister to mum and I would sometimes be present and sit alongside them. They would always leave a copy of the Awake pamphlets and encourage us to read them, which I would. Jane and her husband were so lovely. You could feel the warmth coming from them and over time they actually became friends with mum. The only other times I would attend church was Good Friday with my aunty, siblings and younger cousin. When I started secondary school, dad insisted that both my brother and I attend church. I couldn't understand why as I had never seen him step foot in a church apart from when my aunt got married. We both started to attend a local Catholic church but eventually my brother stopped going as he had football practice. Now thinking back, I think this was his 'get out' clause. I continued going for a while but admittedly it was because I didn't want to get in trouble by dad. However, I did enjoy going and catching up with the other children afterwards. But throughout this time, and if I am honest, I still didn't have a connection with God.

Mum had started attending a Pentecostal church in Brixton and occasionally we would attend. I think it was more out of curiosity as we just wanted to know what was keeping her out so often and why she was so fired up about this 'God'. She found a new church nearer to home and although I would attend church sporadically I didn't take any steps towards being saved.

I remember being in my twenties when I received my first message from God. At that point in my life, I was out having fun, raving most week days and weekends, drinking, smoking, travelling, and simply enjoying being young. One night, I had a dream where a boxing match was taking place. I believe it was Lennox Lewis who was fighting. I honestly can't recall who but it was someone who was well-known at the time. In the dream, I could hear a voice of the boxer saying, "Come into the light, better doth shine." It was early hours of the morning and I woke up out of my sleep, found a piece of paper and pen and wrote those words down. I couldn't quite understand what was going on and why God would speak to me through a dream using boxers. However, it was a message I never forgot and one that, as I grew more in Christ and built upon our relationship, I understood what was meant by it.

After that dream, I continued to lead the same lifestyle, still going out and drinking to the point where I woke up with major hangovers. I swore I would never drink again whilst nursing a sore head yet I repeated the same the following week, if not the next day. I kept running away from God not realising that He was trying to draw me into His light, where there were better things in store for me.

Prior to getting saved in 2003 and having attended church for many years, I just found the whole thing a bit of a farce. I would attend church when I felt like it and would often come away feeling uplifted for a while but didn't really adjust my behaviour. In fact, most of the time I couldn't understand what was going on in the church. People getting overly emotional and shouting 'Hallelujah'. If anything I thought they were just putting on a performance and their behaviour didn't seem genuine. Hearing people speaking in tongues and falling on the floor, which I was told was the Holy Spirit working within them, I thought *if that's what the Holy Spirit does to people then it can leave me alone.* Most times I would be laughing at these people making complete fools of themselves in front of me. Sometimes it was a bit scary only because I didn't understand what was going on. However, I was still drawn to go back and couldn't work out why. What on earth was I searching for?

There was one particular church service I attended where I decided to go up for prayer. On this day I could only say that I was hoodwinked as one minute I was a sinner then the next thing I was being saved. The minister that was leading the service had me and others repeat what he was saying. I had no idea that I was actually making a declaration that I was accepting Jesus as my personal Saviour until it was too late. We were then brought to the pastor's office and given books and welcomed into God's kingdom. Even then I was saying I was saved but did not really believe it. I didn't feel any connection with God and so I continued living my life as before.

The senior pastor of the church would sometimes call me up for prayer as well as other visiting pastors. They would often speak over my life and tell me to accept Christ into my life. I would always refuse but they were persistent and continued to pray for me. Most weeks I attended there was always an altar call. I recall one particular day they did one and I didn't go up as I knew where it would lead to and I just wasn't ready. However, I stood up with the rest of the congregation whilst others were being prayed for. I fixed my eyes on the wall, praying that the pastor would not call me up as I didn't want any attention drawn to me. Sometimes I just wanted to go to church, sink into the background, listen to the word, hear the gospel songs, and then leave. At that point in my life I believed that was enough and all I needed. But it seemed as if God wasn't listening and all of a sudden I felt a hand on my shoulder and could hear the pastor's voice in my ear. I didn't even turn around but just stood there, rolling my eyes, feeling extremely uncomfortable and wishing that she would just go away. When she finished I stayed in the same position not even acknowledging or thanking her for praying for me. I just wanted to be left alone and not forced into this church thing. I can now ask God to forgive me for my behaviour.

I had one foot in and one foot out believing that if I put both feet in that I would have to give up too many of the things that I enjoyed. If I didn't commit to Him then He couldn't be mad at me, but at least by being half way in I was showing willingness. I didn't realise by attending church no matter how little, I was actually taking a step closer to Him and He was drawing nearer to me. I believed that the life I was living was filling the void that I had in my life, helping me to forget about the true feeling of loneliness I was experiencing. My brother and sister both had children and I remember the day my brother told me his partner was pregnant again. Normally I would be so excited for anyone who announced they were having a baby, but here I was in my late twenties, not settled down, no potential partner on the horizon, and I couldn't bring myself to congratulate him. There was also a Christmas when he had called up around midday and I had not too long woken up. We exchanged seasonal greetings and he asked why I was up so late as he had been up at the crack of the dawn with the kids celebrating Christmas. I was feeling so low and responded by saying, "I have no one to wake up for". I remember sitting in the bath later that day and topping up the bath water with my tears. I was fed up of just being an aunty and wanted to share my life with someone experiencing the same feelings that my brother and sister had. I fooled myself into believing that a partner and child would make a difference and that would bring me the joy that I needed.

When I met my daughter's dad, things moved very quickly and before I knew it I was pregnant. Strangely enough, even though we didn't know one another that well, it was as if this was destined to be and we were both extremely happy when I took the test and discovered I was expecting. This man that I had met had apparently been watching me for years as he worked for a courier company at the time and used to deliver parcels to the building I worked at. I had noticed him and thought he was kind of cute but dismissed it thinking I wasn't his type. We never had any eye contact or even exchanged any words with one another. After a while I noticed he stopped coming to the building, and one evening on a night out with friends whilst queuing to get into a club he approached me. Initially, I didn't recognise him until he told me that he used to deliver parcels to my building, so we got talking inside the club, exchanged numbers and eventually started to date. I was pregnant for my 30th birthday and our daughter was born in February 2002, five weeks early. I had pre-eclampsia and at 34 weeks pregnant was admitted into hospital as she had stopped growing. My blood pressure was really high and had to be controlled. After a week there was no improvement and I was given an emergency Caesarean section, where immediately she was taken away from me and put into the neo-natal ward. She stayed for two weeks, with me visiting until she was a decent weight and ready to take home. I honestly couldn't wait for the day.

After she was born, I was so overjoyed at being a parent and having a little family of my own that my outlook completely changed. I now had a purpose to carry on and I thought less about me and more about this precious gift that God had blessed me with. Although I still went out with friends, this became less frequent as I had asked God for a child and He had given me what I wanted, so she was my main priority. I did start to attend church more regularly and we had a blessing take place at what was now becoming my church.

I did believe that with my daughter and a partner that loved me, the void I had experienced over the years had been filled. Yet something still felt like it was missing. I had been looking for other things in the form of relationships with friends and family, alcohol, smoking weed, and clubbing to complete me, but there was still a yearning for something more. I had an amazing family, great friends, a nice car, and I was being well paid at a job with no stress. So what more could I need? What did I need to do to fill that emptiness?

I was still attending church with baby in tow and the thing that turned it around for me was watching my sister at a service make her way to the altar for prayer. The church was packed on this occasion and people were apparently receiving their healing, but I was still hesitant to go up. The lady seated next to me, who has now gone home to the Lord, asked if I would like her to go up with me and once again I refused. I sat there and just continued to watch my sister, who was being spoken to, suddenly drop on the floor as if she had fainted, but was actually being filled with this 'Holy Spirit'. This was when I really believed. I had known her all of my life and knew that she would never put on an act, she had really experienced the presence of God and I wanted to feel that too. Eventually, I made the decision to take a step closer to God and accepted Him into my life as my personal Saviour. Finally, I was saved after searching for that missing piece to complete the puzzle, and entered into His light. I started to delve more into His word and had a yearning to be closer to Him, be used by Him and build a closer relationship with Him.

It took a while before I actually experienced the Holy Spirit truly work within me. I think I was still putting up a good fight and didn't want to be seen as looking foolish to others. The first time this happened to me I was standing up and felt this warm, tingling sensation working through my fingers then start to work its way through the rest of my body. I sat down and closed my eyes not understanding what was going on and the deaconess approached me. She could obviously tell what was going on and just rested her hands on me without saying a word. Eventually the feeling passed but I still didn't fully understand it. It was not until years later that I started to speak in tongues, being given just a few words initially. I thought I was just making these words up, but continued to repeat them over and over asking God to interpret them for me. The words *victory* is mine came into my head.

This took place in 2012, the same year I had gone through my bout of depression and was preparing for my baptism. I kept saying I wanted more of Him and He started to fill me up. I was continuing to grow more and tap into the spirit that was already within me. I would spend ages at home just basking in His presence speaking and even singing in tongues and felt such an inner peace come over me. That is when I started to have more dreams. I mentioned before that I would be woken up in the middle of the night to write songs and send messages. One night whilst asleep, I could hear the words *wake up* and I said in my dream, "Lord can we do this in the morning?" I then felt a tug on my head, pulling me out of my sleep. I was urged by God in those early hours to write a message to someone which I did via email. After completing this task, I went back to sleep and the next day they responded thanking me for the message I had sent. He started to use me just as I had asked.

As time went on, I started to act like one of those people that I used to think were foolish. There I was now shouting 'Hallelujah' at the top of my lungs, running around the church, speaking in tongues, being led to pray for people within the congregation and finally falling on the floor.

I never understood why God was using me in such a way. Someone that didn't feel worthy enough to be used as a vessel to do His work, a person who was still not perfect even though I claimed to be a Christian. But God used me even though I was still broken and He knows that I am willing to look foolish for Him. At times, I would go to church and try to hold back. There I was saying I don't want my make up to smear, I don't want to cry today and please don't let me start speaking in tongues or look like an idiot in front of people. In the beginning, I suppose I was concerned about what people would think but eventually I didn't care as I wasn't there to please people. I was there to worship Him, receive my breakthrough when needed and to perform His works. Sometimes I would try to suppress the Holy Spirit and try to quench it but there were times it would unleash itself no matter how much I tried to fight it. After a while, I chose not to resist it and allowed God to do His works through me becoming more obedient to His direction.

One day I was meant to go up and sing and the service went in a completely different direction. God had spoken to me earlier in the week and whilst praising Him I started to clap my hands and couldn't stop until He told me too. He said he wanted people that would look foolish for Him. I told my story at church and asked the congregation to just clap, the clapping went on for at least ten minutes and I started to sing. Right before my eyes people were receiving their healing and deliverance. A little time after that service, one of the members of the congregation who I had prayed for during the service, spoke to me and said she received healing. She used to get regular injections in her eyes, which she said were very painful and when she went back to the hospital they had told her that the issue she was having with her eyes had fixed itself. She no longer required the injections and believed it was from that service. If I wasn't obedient to what God had asked me to do, then she probably would not have received her healing. I am so glad that I was obedient allowing the Holy Spirt to work through me.

There have been times when I have allowed my circumstances and my flesh to take over. Oftentimes I felt like I was alone in the wilderness.

I felt like God's presence had left me and that He wasn't protecting me as He had promised. Because of these feelings I started to draw away, turning my back on Him, which created a disconnection. My faith would start to depart from me and the void would be there again. This, however, would not be for too long as I knew that without Him I couldn't get through, so would always go back in search of the light.

Coming to the light of the Lord definitely made me shine brighter and although it took me over 30 years, it was all a part of God's plan.

Chapter 19

Be Encouraged

Matthew 9 v 20–22 And behold, a woman who had suffered from a discharge of blood for twelve years came up behind him and touched the fringe of his garment, for she said to herself, "If I only touch his garment, I will be made well." Jesus turned, and seeing her he said, "Take heart, daughter; your faith has made you well." And instantly the woman was made well. (ESV)

The path that you walk through in life is not always determined by you. Your life is preordained by God. No matter how much you try to veer from that life and try to change it, it only takes you a little longer to reach your destination. The best thing to do is not fight it or struggle trying to make it what you feel it ought to be. Let go and let God do His work. He is the author and finisher of all things.

We are the ones that put limitations on ourselves and God will use us in spite of what we believe to be weaknesses. So, we need to stop condemning ourselves if we are children of God. Romans 8 v 1 says – *There is therefore now no condemnation to them which are in Christ Jesus, who walk not after the flesh, but after the spirit (KJV).* Therefore we are to be led by the spirit and not of the flesh.

God chose people with weaknesses such as Jeremiah who deemed himself as being too young, however became a prophet to the nation; and Moses who had a speech impediment yet led the people out of Egypt. He chose these people to accomplish great things. God sees your potential. Focus on who God says you are and if you are unsure and need reminding there are several descriptions within the Bible.

You can see that over the years I have gone through times when I have felt completely broken but on my journey as a Christian I have been able to discover many new things about myself and have grown spiritually. This chapter highlights some of the things I have learnt and also what stage I am at in my journey.

I received the joy I had been yearning for over many years and experienced it in a way I had never felt before. There are still bad days where I don't always feel upbeat but I constantly strive to get back to that place of Joy. The inner peace was received and I stopped fretting about insignificant things but began to feel content with my circumstances knowing that God was in control. I found strength in my weakness and refused to stay in low places, no longer accepting defeat as my portion. Although it has been a long hard battle, I know how strong I truly am. The joy of the Lord was my strength; throughout my difficulties He has been with me. The chains/stronghold around my feet and neck were broken as I no longer chose to live in the past or hold onto past hurts. I have been cleansed and renewed, no longer holding myself in captivity, escaping from the cage and now having a clearer vision. I understand that changing my mindset, not being so hard on myself or expecting too much from others, will free me from disappointment. *Medonoya* means "renewing of the mind" and although difficult to do at times, this has helped me on my journey by looking at things from a new perspective. My outlook on life is more positive and I now view myself differently, loving myself more, accepting who I was before and who I am now. I recognise that I am a living creation of God and He lives within me. Therefore, if I say I love Him, I have to love myself and shouldn't seek anyone's approval but God's. I am blessed and highly favoured as the Word says. I recognise that I have been more fortunate than others in the sense that my journey has not been as tough as theirs and I am grateful that God has had a hand in this, therefore I am content with who I am and where I am.

I have been the sole carer for my daughter from the beginning having to deal with day-to-day issues on my own. Even though I didn't want the situation to be that way, especially being brought up in a single parent home, I was fighting so hard to make a difference. I became increasingly frustrated when it didn't work out with her dad, feeling that I had failed, and put a lot of pressure on myself to be the best mother I could be. I have now accepted the situation and recognise that I have done a good job in raising her and shouldn't feel that I have let her down by things not working out with her father. He also needs to be accountable for this situation and although we both believed we were ready to be parents, he wasn't ready to take on the full responsibility that comes with it which was being committed to both of us. Don't get me wrong he has been there and his relationship with our daughter is brilliant. But being a single parent, we cannot just switch off and sometimes I felt that he didn't always make her his top priority so I was resentful at times. We have, however, tried to bring our daughter up in as stable an environment and I realise that continuing to apportion blame will not benefit either of us or change the circumstances. I am not going to overcompensate for her dad not being there 24/7 but I am definitely aware of how this situation may affect her at times. My mother has also helped me by setting the standards, giving me the ideals to live by to help shape and create a loving environment for my daughter; a place where she feels safe and is able to come and share with me her inner most fears and knows that she is protected at all times. Not only by me but also with God.

Anger was one of my main issues and although it is okay to be angry at times, I have learnt not to let it control my life. I recognised that I was angry for a long time and where this had stemmed from. It was very deep rooted but I allowed myself to delve deeper, even if it was painful. This introspection helped me to accept certain things which, in turn, has allowed me to move forward. The counselling sessions have made me look back on my life and helped me to figure out where the anger came from. Sometimes you know the answers already, but you are just afraid to start digging around in the past. My childhood was not a particularly great one and most definitely wasn't as bad as some, however, I have learnt not to discount my life or my feelings. I suffered abuse, bullying, loneliness and the feelings of being rejected by my father and others. I was never able to discuss this with anyone so I started to put up a façade and tried to block everything out. I was never able to really trust anyone enough to disclose what I was going through. Unfortunately, I turned it all around becoming a bully, the angry, ignorant person that people should fear. I became the troublemaker but in actual fact that behaviour was really my way of crying out for help. No one recognised it, so it just got worse. People just began to expect that from me and held the opinion that I was the one who wouldn't take any mess, which was so far from the truth because that was all I was taking. So much so that I even started to create more mess for myself as I was so confused. I couldn't always tell the difference between right and wrong. I always wanted to be liked and accepted by people so I gave in a lot to peer pressure and in turn had to keep up this façade.

From a young age, I was never really in control of what happened in my life so I thought the only way to regain that control was to become the aggressor. I then started using this technique by being forceful, aggressive and acting as if I didn't care which I believed would create the desired effect. This nonchalant attitude I carried was so far from the real me. I would act out and become angry or disappointed when things didn't go the way I had planned. I felt that was the way to be because then people wouldn't be able to take advantage of me and I wouldn't get hurt. By putting up a defence mechanism, I would be in charge and have control over what happened to me. But I have learnt that you cannot have total control of what happens to you. Only God knows the plans that He has in store for you therefore hand the controls over to Him and allow Him to guide and direct you.

As you know, I started smoking and drinking in my teens and my behaviour was sometimes irrational and aggressive. This I now know is because I internalised a lot of things rather than releasing them, and when it became too much, I was like a volcano spewing out hot lava everywhere. This still happens sometimes, but I am learning to control the eruptions and trying to channel my feelings in a different way, so they are becoming less frequent. For example, now I think before speaking, predicting what the outcome may be, weighing up the options, and getting my point across in a more controlled way. Maintaining a more relaxed and calm approach, letting trivial things not become such a big issue and most importantly looking to God for guidance.

Trusting people that come into my life has been difficult as oftentimes when I have trusted them they have let me down. When I feel that my trust has been abused, I begin to shut down and withdraw myself from them, i.e. men, friends and family. I felt that my father had let me down from a very young age and I couldn't trust him to stick around for very long. He wasn't around for my birth up to seven years old. I then spent the next seven years of my life building a relationship with him believing that he was going to be around for good and from the age of fourteen he deserted me again. So I suppose I always started to expect the worst; when I did have a glimmer of hope that things would be good, it would always end up with someone hurting me and letting me down again. Relationships with guys were messed up, after being let down on numerous occasions and being cheated on. I would then begin to build myself up again, find the strength and invest my trust into someone and eventually the same cycle would recur. Friends, were pretty much the same and I couldn't hold onto them for very long. I felt like I was giving so much yet not getting back much in return. Eventually, this would damage the relationship especially when I felt they were taking advantage of my good nature. Some family members would also do the same so I started to withdraw from everyone and never fully opened myself up. I made them believe what they wanted to believe, which was that I was the angry, ignorant, miserable person. This then affected my personality and made me very wary of people. But underneath I have a good heart which was gradually being broken. I began to believe that it was all my fault but I have learnt that people will let you down and that they, too, should be accountable for their actions. People aren't always going to do things the way you want them to or to your liking and these things will build your character and give you a better understanding not only of who you are but of who they are. In this way, you can allow relationships to grow. Don't judge people by your own standards because each of us sees, experiences and relates to the world differently. My relationship with my dad has changed and I do not allow the past to dictate what happens in future. I have learnt to love and accept him for who he is. By not expecting too much from people you will not be disappointed.

Jealousy has been an area I have struggled with for a long time and believe that this could also be connected to me not feeling in control. I may have acted jealously when I felt I was not in control of a situation/person. As mentioned before I have always been very protective of other people in my life and sometimes I feel threatened when someone else can come in and take away the people that I love or hold dear to me. I wouldn't say I deem the individuals as my possession, but they are/were the people that I depend(ed) upon to not let me down. I would then become enraged when I felt that someone may be encroaching upon our relationship and somehow try to alter it. Now this doesn't just ring true for the relationships with guys, it's also includes my family. I remember when my sister used to meet guys when I was younger, I didn't want her to be around them because I felt they would eventually take her away from me. Even when my brother's ex-girlfriend started to form a relationship with my mum after I left home, I was convinced that she was trying to replace me. I started to get extremely irritated and acted quite childishly if I am perfectly honest. I know this was not to be true, but I still couldn't help acting upon my emotions, so much so that it got to the point that mum had to reassure me that I couldn't be replaced. I believe this behaviour was because I haven't had much confidence in myself and always expect people to walk away from me. The insecurity creeps in because I've found it difficult to trust anyone and by trying to grab on to the person it could often drive them away. I just need to remember that I cannot control a situation no matter what I do. I need to be more in control of my emotions and rebuild the confidence within myself and understand that I don't own anyone.

Broken, Not Beyond Repair | Karen Holder

I am learning how to love and respect myself more and although it is something I have been aware of for a long time, I was still looking for other people to complete me. I have to love myself and all my faults and in loving myself I will become happier with who I am, accepting that I am significant and worthy of love and not being so hard on myself when things don't go according to plan. In the past, this would have made me feel like a failure. Now I recognise that I did my best through these situations and nothing beats a failure but a try. I am becoming more comfortable with myself and understanding who Karen Holder really is. This, in turn, is making me stronger and more determined and is teaching me that others' opinions of me are not what really matter. It's more important how I view myself. I had been looking for men to make me happy and figured that if someone could love and respect me then I would be able to love myself in return, which was definitely the wrong approach. God has taught me that it is not impossible to love again even if you have been hurt, but if you are strong in who you are and begin to love and value yourself, the love will start to flow from other places. I honestly believe this to be true and realise that I do have something of value to bring to people and I am important. People do look up to me and see me as an encourager and an inspiration although I never thought it possible. This is due to the fact that I had no faith or confidence in myself most of the time. It was all a façade as I never actually believed in me.

I have let go of the guilt that I have been feeling for so long and I'm learning to be accountable for only the things that I have done, not letting this emotion hang over me. I will no longer beat myself up and refuse to hang onto the past or my failings and acknowledge that things don't always go according to plan. Over time, I have noticed that people try to turn situations around on me when they are feeling guilty about their behaviour or actions. No one wants to accept that they are wrong and are always looking for a scapegoat to push things onto as they don't want to be accountable or take responsibility for their errors. I used to hold their guilt and try to make amends even if I knew I wasn't in the wrong. This is where the whole accountability issue comes in and I should only be accountable for what I have done, recognise my wrongdoings and not allow others to transfer their guilt onto me.

Have faith and know God is so important no matter what you are going through. God has truly been an essential part of my life and has allowed me to accept a lot of things and believe in myself again. I had been yearning for Him for such a long time and wasn't even aware that He was the piece that was missing in my broken puzzle. But now He is in my life, I understand just what it was that was missing. He has made me accept a lot of things and has lightened the burdens that I have been carrying just by putting my faith and trust in Him. God has helped me to change my outlook and my attitude towards life so I am so grateful that I have allowed Him back into my life. Without God guiding, comforting and protecting me, I would still be on the path of destruction. Whenever things get me down I just remember to praise His name and know that things will change. Thank you Lord!

If there is something you can do about a situation, do it. If there is nothing you can do about it, pray through it.

Therefore, be encouraged that God can come into your life just like the woman in Matthew 9 v 20–22. Having struggled with her issue for 12 years, she was determined to touch him that she would be healed. This woman pressed through the tight crowd with a faith so strong that she believed He would heal her. Never give up but continue to pursue God through prayer, seeking him throughout the difficult moments and He will deliver you.

Conclusion

Don't look at a setback as a problem, rather see it as an opportunity to reflect, get back up and perform even better than before.

I can honestly say that my journey hasn't been an easy one and that I am now living a perfect life. My journey shall continue and I am certain that along the way I will still come across many obstacles. Trying to stay aligned with God, however, has helped me to get to the place I am so far. My approach has changed in the way that I have dealt with situations and people which has not been without His guidance and Him allowing me to look at things from a new perspective.

I have achieved so much and have yet to achieve more; I have finally been able to release all the things that have been a hindrance and burden to me which has helped me to find a new confidence from within. I am now starting to bloom and am very proud of the progress I have made so far by choosing not to give up but by being determined to push through. This new confidence has revealed to me how much potential and amazing talents God has blessed me with and wants me to use.

Nothing is guaranteed in life and as much as we would like to be in control, planning how our lives should be or even look we honestly don't know what the future has in store for us. But we must not let the past dictate the future and should break free from the chains that are restricting us. I have faith that God will bring me through all situations or problems that may occur which I do not have control over. I know that He will make them right if I just allow Him to take over. By giving God the control over me I can my see my purpose more clearly. God is making the way and opening doors for me and my only purpose is to please Him whilst I am alive on this Earth. Even though I cannot see as far ahead as He can, I know that He has my best interests at heart.

As I mentioned earlier, I am far from perfect. Although we are born perfect, innocent and pure, the world we are living in can taint us. The images that we see and the experiences we have from childhood to adulthood have a huge impact on our behaviour and the way we view things. As Christians we can constantly be in conflict with our inner man (the holy spirit) and outer man (the flesh). The inner man is one of peace, perfection and purity. By viewing things from a spiritual perspective and allowing God to work through us, we can reap the benefits bringing us closer to perfection.

Think about the things that you can handle and God can handle. Cast all your burdens onto Him such as loneliness, anger, stress, anxiety, and impatience. Relief doesn't always come quickly but life isn't easy and the issues we face on a daily basis can become overwhelming. Life is like a playing field and the more we take part in the game and practice, the better we become at it. We just have to play the best game with the knowledge we have. God can give you that knowledge and the more we are with Him and have Him on our side the better we become at dealing with these issues and will win the game. God is the best player to have on your team. In fact, He can be the player, the coach and the entire team if you need Him to be.

Look at what is good about you. There is a lot to be admired and, most importantly, never forget that you are a child of the Most High God. God calls you a masterpiece, you have been created by God almighty and He formed you in your mother's womb. Always speak positivity into your life and continually accept and approve yourself. God doesn't make any mistakes and you have been fearfully and wonderfully made.

There is a part of you that is perfect and pure. It is untouched by the less than perfect characteristics you have acquired by living in a less than perfect world. This part of you is a still and eternal star. Make time to reach it and this will bring you untold benefit. (Bramah Kumaris, Spiritual Organisation)

Rekindle your relationship with God and let him reignite the fire and allow your eternal star to shine brighter.

I pray that this book has helped you in some way and equipped you with the knowledge that even though you may feel broken you are most definitely not beyond repair.

I shall continue on my journey, uncertain of which direction or path my life will take but always trusting that God will be with me comforting, strengthening, carrying and repairing me along the way.

About the Author

Karen Holder is a mother, born to West Indian parents and has lived in London all of her life. Like many, she has faced a number of adversities over the years and has had to call on her courageous and tenacious spirit to overcome them. However, it is really her strong belief in God and her firm relationship with Him that has helped guide Karen to walk a path of spiritual enlightenment. Her relationship with God has played a pivotal role not only in her personal and spiritual transformation but in her decision to write a book and share her experiences with others with the intention of helping those wherever possible.

Karen has shared the experiences of her life and been very open with readers. She feels that it is important to be honest about her journey and the struggles she has faced from childhood to date, as well as dealing with those battles from the perspective of a Christian woman.

Karen has a fun-loving character and, on many occasions, has been told that her smile can brighten up a room, however, underneath that smile, is a woman who was at one time in need of help, struggling with depression and low self-esteem. She now knows that her experiences were for a purpose, which is to help and encourage others to see that there is always hope and that they, too, can overcome life's challenges.

Her passion is motivating people to see their worth and bringing attention to the talents they may not recognise in themselves. She wants to help people build upon their abilities and unique qualities, supporting and inspiring them on their journey to peace and joy and enabling them to fulfil their potential, passion and purpose.

Currently working within the Project Management industry, Karen also has a creative flair and enjoys writing poetry. She has dreamed of having her work published or recognised and felt inspired to write and share *Broken, Not Beyond Repair*. She believes that everyone has the potential to change and that no matter what circumstances have afflicted them in the past, they can still create a better future and live out their dreams.

Lightning Source UK Ltd.
Milton Keynes UK
UKHW02f1831050718

325295UK00012B/644/P